AF568060

FRUSTRATION OF PROSPECTIVE TEACHERS

FRUSTRATION
OF
PROSPECTIVE TEACHERS

By

Vempati Roja Ramani

M.A., M.Ed.

Lecturer, College of Education

Guntur, Andhra Pradesh

Editor

Dr. Digumarti Bhaskara Rao

M.Sc., M.A., M.A., M.Ed., Ph.D.

Reader & Research Director

R.V.R. College of Education

Srinivasa Nagar Colony

Guntur – 522006, A.P.

digumartibhaskararao@rediffmail.com

DISCOVERY PUBLISHING HOUSE PVT. LTD.

NEW DELHI-110 002

First Published-2009

ISBN 978-81-8356-377-2

Published by

DISCOVERY PUBLISHING HOUSE PVT. LTD.
4831/24, Ansari Road, Prahlad Street
Darya Ganj, New Delhi-110002 (India)
Phone: 23279245 • Fax: 91-11-23253475
E-mail: dphbooks@rediffmail.com
dphtemp@indiatimes.com
website: www.discoverypublishing.com

Printed at:

Sachin Printers
Delhi

Dedicated
to
Dr. Kilari Sunil Kumar,
Dr. Kilari (Chandra) Radhika
in recognition of their
excellent Medical Service

Preface

The human individuals try to fulfill their needs in order to live happily and function effectively, but these needs can not always be adequately satisfied on account of several obstacles and obstructions. These obstructions cause frustration and produce tension. Frustration is an emotion that occurs in situations, where one is blocked from reaching a personal goal. In today's competitive scenario, every person has his targets that he wanted to achieve timely and if he is not able to achieve his targets he is frustrated. Warning signs to frustration are shortness of breath, knot in the throat, stomach cramps, chest pains, headache, excessive alcohol consumption, increased smoking, lack of patience, desire to strike out, etc.

The frustration can affect the mind in a negative way in which person's thinking power gets slowed down. Frustration leads a person take wrong decisions and as a result of which he is not able to come with innovative ideas. He is not able to achieve all his targets and is left with only his uncompleted plans and unachieved targets. Such a frustrated person goes far away from reality.

The present study is intended to find out the level of frustration of prospective teachers. The prospective teachers studying in Colleges of Education are with an average level of frustration. Except teaching methodology, the gender, the locality, and the qualification of prospective teachers did not show any influence on the level of frustration of prospective teachers.

The prospective teachers should learn to recognise the warning signs of frustration, intervene to calm themselves down physically, modify their thoughts in a way that reduce their stress, fix goals as per their abilities and necessities, learn to communicate assertively, and dare to ask for help in order to prevent frustration.

This study would be of great use to planners and administrators of teacher education and heads of teacher education institutions along with parents and society.

Dr. D. Bhaskara Rao

Sri Sai Soudha
D-43, S.V.N. Colony
Guntur 522006
A.P., India

Contents

1

Introduction

"Education is the conscious and deliberate process in which one personality acts upon another in order to modify the development of the other by the communication and manipulation of knowledge."

—John Adams

"Life presents a continuous chain of struggle for existence and survival", says Darwin. Everyone strives hard for the satisfaction of his needs. In struggling to achieve something if one finds that results are not satisfactory, one either changes one's goals or the procedure. Human situations and environment conditions are in changing phenomena. An individual is confronted with new conditions and problems of life from the very infancy up to death and he is constantly busy with finding satisfactory and pleasure giving solutions by using his inherent intelligence and other gifted capacities of the mind and the body.

Human being is in constant conflict with his environment. This is a distinctive feature of all living beings. Consequently, every living being tries to achieve some working arrangement and adjustment with his environment in order to carry on with his life despite of various conflicts. Adjustment, therefore, is an important factor in the life of all living beings. Not only normal beings but even the individuals who are abnormal and insane try to find out some sort of working arrangement or adjustment with their environment.

A person does not always get success according to his desires and efforts. The reason for not getting success lies either in unfavourable situations or in limited capacities of the individual. However, a person makes efforts to adjust himself somehow in his environment. In these efforts, sometimes, he achieves full success and sometimes only partial. On achieving partial success, a person tries to find other means of adjustment. When he fails in this effort, he does not find himself adjusted. In this situation, abnormality appears in his behaviour. Abnormality points out towards some mental illness or worry. (S.P. Choube)

Herbert Spencer defined 'life' as 'the continuous adjustment of the internal to the external relations'. This leads itself to the suggestion that life is always modified to fit external circumstance and ignores the essence of civilisation, which is modification of the external world to suit man's internal needs and desires. Every individual has some specific and definite needs that he extremely desires to fulfill, and every individual has to live in certain specific environmental conditions in which these desires are fulfilled.

If the conditions are favourable, no particular difficulty is felt in case of every individual that his conditions may be favourable to the fulfillment of his needs. Every individual in his life has to face some conditions that are not inclined to show favour to the fulfillment of some of his needs. Such conditions act as impediments and always prove obstacles in the way of fulfillment of these needs and in this way create problems and difficulties.

Man is ambitious by nature. He has so many aspirations and desires to be fulfilled. He plans and strives hard for their realisation but it may be possible that despite his best planning and efforts he may not get the desired success. At times, he finds himself to the state of utter confusion and bewilderment. All the paths for going a head seem to be blocked. This sort of affaires along with the repeated failure in the attempts put one into a state or condition that refers to failure to satisfy a basic need because of either condition in the individual or external obstacles. (S.K. Mangal)

In the background of human behaviour, a type of internal feeling works to motivate a person for activity in certain direction. Actually, by this motive power, a man always tries to achieve the desired goal.

But, it is also true that an individual always can not achieve the desired goal because several barriers of environment come in his way towards the goal. In addition to these there are several other motives to be satisfied which the individual can not do due to one or the other reason. This unsatisfied motives lead to conflict or frustrations in an individual. These frustrated situations of various types, occurring at the same time in front of an individual, ultimately leads to abnormality, which is psychologically termed as stress. (Govind Tiwari)

Frustration is a state of hopelessness and disgust. When there is frustration in a person's life, his enthusiasm is gone, tension in his life and mind is increased and often he overcomes by total despair and dejection. Frustration also increases aggression and the variability experiences some obstacles real or imagined between him and his goal. Frustration, therefore, is a mental condition which a natural consequence of our failure to satisfy some motive or desire. (Tiwari)

A frustrated state of mind exhibits extreme tension, lack of peace, sense of inferiority, etc., besides much kind of mental mechanism functions in the state of frustration. Frustration is a feeling caused by the inhibition of desires and or a threat to a person's self concept when a child is forbidden to achieve a goal, restricted from an activity or insulted by another person, he may become frustrated. Frustration may also be brought about by an inner conflict between conscience and desire, or by the persons own inability to complete the task. (Govind)

Aggressive behaviour in individuals has often been explained as the manifestations of deep seated frustrations. People differ in their capacity to withstand the frustrating situations. It is very important to note that even after an emotional flare-up of optimum intensity, the frustration prolific situation mostly remains unchanged. So, while meeting these frustrating situations we should not be explosive since it bears no impact in ameliorating the same. (K.K. Bhatia and K.C. Behera)

Our frustrations may be caused by minor obstacles in the environment, by conflicts with other people, by environmental situations beyond our control, by economic deprivation, by social customs, traditions and taboos, by the exaggeration of our personal deficiencies and by conflicts of motives within ourselves. (B. Kuppu Swamy)

Lack of opportunities, delays, discriminatory treatment, lack of resources, etc., are some of the other factors involved in frustration. It has been found that stress related symptoms like diabetics, hypertension, ulcers, etc. also cause frustration. The pressure to go after success endlessly, ultimately results in stress which manifests itself in various forms like regression, aggression, resignation and fixation.

Frustration and conflict, the two forms of thwarting are closely related. Normally, when frustration results from some obstruction, the organism involved is seen adopting aggressive and violent behaviour towards the obstacle. Such aggressive behaviour can be direct as well as indirect. In children and unintelligent people, it takes a direct form; while in the case of most adults and intelligent people, it takes a more indirect manifestation. Now, if the child's normal expression of aggressive and violence resulting from some form of frustration is curbed and restricted, then it is actually prevented, but at the same time it becomes repressed and gives rise to feelings of fear and insecurity. Thus, some people become violent on being faced with some frustrating feelings of fear and insecurity as a result of the curb on their aggressive behaviour. As to the mode of behaviour that should be adopted in dealing with obstacles that cause frustration, an individual learns through trail and error. Different situations and circumstances find him behaving difficulty and the behaviour patterns of adjustment that satisfy him are repeated while the patterns that cause him displeasure are discarded and replaced. And, the various reactions concerning the adjustment to different frustrations gradually take on the form of habits. Hence, adult individuals display permanent individual difference in the patterns of adjustment. (Sharma and Kumar)

A frustrated individual who cannot create or find a means to reduce his frustration may become deeply trouble. Most of us sense this in ourselves and try to find a satisfactory substitute for unrealised goals. To adjust, we must deal successfully with frustration. Frustration does not always lead to aggressive behaviour, but aggressive responses will tend to persist or recur if they help us to reach our goals. (Robert E. Silverman)

Frustration, however, is a necessary experience in the half of any child and adult, a necessary accompaniment of the processes of growing up. It can stimulate greater efforts at productivity and creativity, if it is not in excess and if we have developed the ability to tolerate frustration. This ability is called frustration-tolerance. (B. K. Swamy)

STATEMENT OF THE PROBLEM

A Study of Frustration of Prospective Teachers.

NEED OF THE STUDY

Health problems may arise due to incompatibility between the demands of the educational system and the characteristics of learner or between learner's expectations and the educational processes or both. Such incompatibilities are becoming more and more salient in the context of increasing competition in the job market, increased pressure for achievement from parents, uncertain future and parental aspirations and their desire for compensation through their progeny.

Failure in examination, underachievement and the resulting frustration are becoming prominent features of educational life at school as well as at the higher educational levels, leading a wide range of health problems having far reaching consequences for individual as well as society well-being. This is reflected in a recent analysis of suicide among students. Since the course which they are studying is only one year but the syllabus and the project works to be completed are many, the prospective teachers are more anxious in completing their project works in time, the failure of which results in them more frustration about future examinations, for which they have to cover a lot of syllabus. They are more frustrated about their future plans since each and every prospective teacher who is in a queue of completing the B.Ed. course will be waiting for a job notification through which they can get a government job.

So, teacher educators, administrators, policy planners and guidance personnel connected with teacher education programmes, should think of ways and means of reducing the level of frustration among the teacher trainees, so that they can perform still better to improve the qualities among their students when they join the teacher education course.

SCOPE OF THE STUDY

The present study is confined to the Guntur district. The sample selected for the study was prospective teachers, who were studying in Colleges of Education and the sample size chosen for the present study was 300 (three hundred) prospective teachers only.

The variables chosen for the study were gender (male and female), locality (rural and urban), teaching methodology (arts and science), and educational qualification (graduation and post-graduation).

The other factors that are contributing to the present study are age, adjustment, mental health, retention, working and non-working women, etc., are not taken because of time and money, and hence the researcher has confined the study to only four variables, namely, gender, locality, teaching methodology of study and educational qualification of the prospective teachers.

OBJECTIVES OF THE STUDY

The objectives of the study were:

1. To find out the frustration of prospective teachers;
2. To compare the frustration of male and female prospective teachers;
3. To compare the frustration of rural and urban prospective teachers;
4. To compare the frustration of arts and science prospective teachers;
5. To compare the frustration of graduate and post-graduate prospective teachers.

EDUCATIONAL IMPLICATIONS

The present study helps the people and personnel involved in teacher education, in reducing the frustration of prospective teachers if found it in them. It also helps in devising suitable strategies and programmes either to avoid or reduce frustration. If frustration avoiding and reducing strategies and programmes are informed to prospective teachers, they will implement them in classrooms when they become teachers.

2

Review of Related Literature

"If we fail to build the foundation of knowledge provided by the review of literature our work is likely to be shallow, and will often be a duplicate work that has already been done by some one else."

—W.R. Borg

Any worthwhile research study in any field of knowledge requires an adequate familiarity with the work which has already been done in the same area. A summary of the writings of recognised authorities and of previous research provides evidence that the research is familiar with what is already known and what is still unknown and untested. Since effective research is based upon past knowledge, this step helps to eliminate the duplication of what has been done, and provides useful hypotheses and helpful suggestions for significant investigation.

Citing studies that show substantial agreement and those that seem to present conflicting conclusions help to sharpen and define understanding of existing knowledge in the problem area, provide a background for the research project and make the reader aware of the status of the issue. Parading a long list of annotated studies related to the problem is ineffective and inappropriate. Only those studies that are plainly relevant, competently executed and clearly reported should be included. (Digumarti Bhaskara Rao, 1997)

Capitalising on the reviews of expert researchers can be fruitful in providing helpful ideas and suggestions. While review articles that summarised related studies are useful, they do not provide a satisfactory substitute for an independent research. Even though the review of related literature is not a substitute for an independent work, it is one of the first steps in the research process. It is a valuable guide to define the problem, to recognise its significance, to suggest promising data-gathering devices, to appropriate study design and sources of data for effective analysis and to arrive at fruitful conclusions. (Digumarti Bhaskara Rao, 1999)

The need and importance of related studies and literature have been highlighted by Best who says: "particularly all human knowledge can be found in books and libraries" unlike other animals that most start a new with each generation, man builds upon the accumulated and recorded knowledge of the past.

Dewey has outlined review of related studies as the third step of the scientific method. It is a crucial step which invariably minimises the risk of dead ends, rejected topics, rejected studies, wasted efforts, trail and error activity extended towards approaches already discarded by previous investigations and even more important erroneous findings based on the faulty research design.

The survey of related literature and studies also helps to avoid the risk of duplication. It helps the investigator to see whether the evidence already available solves the problem adequately without further investigation, thus to avoid the risk of duplication.

Though the search for related literature is a time consuming process, it is necessary for a good research. Hence, this study.

THEORETICAL PERSPECTIVES

Here, the theoretical concepts related frustrations will be viewed clearly so as to have a clear idea about frustration.

I. Origin of the Word Frustration

Freud, in his article "My views on the part played by sexuality in the Etiology of Neuroses" (1906), referred to frustrated excitation. He used the word "FRUSTRANE", a word probably formed from the

German verb "frustriern" (to frustrate), that was in every day usage. The German language has no equivalent to the substantive form "frustration", which was later used in English.

Freud, in his article "Types of Onset of Neurosis" (1912), described frustration as the cause, both internal and external, for Neurosis.

In the view of English-language authors, Melanie Klein in particular, frustration incites the reality principle and modulates psychic functioning.

Jean Michel Petot (1982) suggested that the English term "deprivation" was closer to the German versagung.

II. A View of Frustration

When someone is prevented from satisfying a need or desire, we say that frustration has occurred. If people are planning an outing and if rains, they probably experience mild, temporary frustration. The adverse weather is a barrier that prevents them from reaching their goal, having a picnic outdoors.

External as well as internal barriers produce frustration. Some external barriers, such as floods, power failures, transportation, breakdowns, etc., are non-social. Internal barriers are personal limitations and disabilities that thwart one's aspirations, weaknesses, unattractiveness, lack of skill, low intelligence may stand in the way of achievement.

Objects and events become barriers to adjustment only when they block goals which the individual has set and when the individual is aware that they impede his progress toward these goals.

The process of encountering and dealing with barriers has been described in terms of sequence of motivated behaviour. (Norman L. Munn, L. Dodge Fernald and Peter S. Fernald)

The feelings, thoughts and behaviours associated with not achieving a particular goal or the belief that a goal has been prematurely interrupted can develop frustration.

In every ten people, seven are affected by it and out of them three are severely affected. It is a mental feeling that is growing like other dangerous diseases such as AIDS.

III. Meaning of Frustration

A feeling of discomfort, disappointment or insecurity aroused by a blocking of gratification or by the existence of unresolved problems is referred to as frustration.

Frustration is an emotion that occurs in situations, where one is blocked from reaching a personal goal. The more important is the goal the greater the frustration. It is comparable to anger.

Frustration is a feeling of disappointment and discomfort aroused in the mind of human beings only when something has went wrong with them or they are not able to achieve the goals that they had set for themselves.

The word frustration, now in common usage, refers to the state of someone who denies himself, or who is denied, the drive of satisfaction.

Frustration is a human emotion that occurs in situations where one's goals remain unreachable indefinitely. These goals are important to a person and one holds on to them despite their elusiveness.

Failure to affirm ones own essence is simply another name for frustration. Its non-fulfillment of one's efforts to do the best, the withering of one's faculties, is the stunting of one's personality.

Frustration is that state of organism resulting when the satisfaction of motivated behaviour is rendered difficult or impossible.

Generally, frustration is considered with three meanings which are related to its various fields (J.C. Coleman, 1971):

(i) *Frustrating Situation:* Brown and Farber (1951), Lawson and Marx (1958), Amsel (1958, 1962) are of the view that following are the frustrating situations—situations which have partial or total physical barriers, in which the reward is reduced or over, the response is delayed when success is expected but failure or punishment is received;

(ii) *Frustrating State:* Frustrating situations drive the person to the frustrating state. The degree of frustrating state depends upon the power of situation. More powerful situation produces more frustration. Various frustrating situations produce various degrees of frustration in different people. Quantitative and direct measure of frustrating state is possible. It is measured by G.S.R. activity and pulse rate;

(iii) *Reaction to Frustration:* The reactions of frustration is: aggression, regression and fixation. On the basis of the above given description, we can say that frustration is not only failure of needs and wishes, but frustration means much more than this.

In our every day life, we come across to many difficult and problematic situations that disturb us tremendously. The origin of all these adverse situations is both the environment and our personal limitations. To restore mental equilibrium in such awkward situations, we try our best. In many cases, our endeavours fail to succeed by deflating the disturbing situations. Our proceeding is blocked by some barriers and we feel frustrated. (K.K. Bhatia and K.K. Behera)

Conflict with various factors in the environment in search of satisfaction for one's desires is a normal condition of human life. No man in the world can entirely fulfill his desires. Failure in the satisfaction of some desires is normal in every person's life, and the path of satisfaction of most of our motives is marred by obstacles and troubles. Naturally, our desires or motives remain unsatisfied on this account. Frustration is the natural consequence of such a difficulty. It is a state of hopelessness and disgust. It destroys a person's enthusiasm, his tension in life is increased and sometimes he becomes victim of complete despair. Thus, frustration is a mental condition which is resultant upon our failure to satisfy some of our motives. The important characteristics of a frustrated state of mind are: extreme tension, sense of inferiority, lack of peace, and various kinds of mental mechanisms. (Ramanath Sarma)

IV. Definitions of Frustration

A frustration is the condition of being thwarted in the satisfaction of a motive. (Carroll)

Frustration means emotional tension resulting from the blocking of a desire or need. (Good)

Frustration is the feeling of being blocked or thwarted in satisfying a need or attaining a goal that the individual perceives as significant. (Kolesnik)

When there is some interference with our goal directed behaviour, the result is frustration. (Gilmer)

Frustration results when our motives are thwarted, either by some obstacle that blocks or impedes our progress toward a desired goal, or by the absence of an appropriate goal. (Coleman)

Frustration is the unpleasant feelings that result when motive satisfaction is blocked or delayed. (S.S. Chauhan)

Frustration refers to failure to satisfy a basic need because of either condition in the individual or external obstacles. (Barney and Lehner)

Frustration essentially belongs to the realm of protest. It relates to something that is desired and not possessed but that is desired without reference to any possibility of gratification or acquisition. (Lacan)

Our frustration is greater when we have much and want more than when we have nothing and want some. We are less dissatisfied when we lack many things than when we seem to lack but one thing. (Eric Hoffer)

A belief in hell and the knowledge that every ambition is doomed to frustration at the hands of a skeleton have never prevented the majority of human beings from behaving as though death were no more than an unfounded rumour. (Aldous Huxley)

I share their frustration at times and I get down just like them when we suffer a bad result. (Steven Gerrad)

I can remember the frustration of not being able to talk. I knew what I wanted to say, but I could not get the words out, so I would just scream. (Temple Grandin)

Frustration is a term used in the physics of spin glasses and also applied to interactions in some types of neural networks, indicating the tendency for conflicting demands to be placed on spin or neuronal interactions.

Frustration is a feeling of discomfort, disappointment, or insecurity aroused by a blocking of gratification or by the existence of unresolved problems.

Frustration, although quite painful at times, is a very positive and essential part of success. (Bennett)

V. Nature of Frustration

As earlier stated, all human behaviour is the result of motivation. Due to motivation, goal-directed behaviour occurs but when the goal-directed behaviour suffers from interferences or barriers, then it results in frustration. The concept of 'frustration' is an important phenomenon particularly in studying the abnormal persons. The frustration process produces behaviour that is purely an end in itself and not a means to an end. The behaviour thus elicited is not an expression of a preference since it is not influenced by what it accomplishes. In this sense, the behaviour is compulsive in nature, and the type of behaviour that is selected in frustration is a matter of its availability at the time as well as a number of other factors not yet clearly understood. This type of behaviour is most readily altered by a reduction in a state of frustration (Maier, N.R.F., 1949). Frustrations occur when one's strivings are thwarted either by obstacles that block progress toward a desired goal or by absence of an appropriate goal. A wide range of obstacles, both environmental and internal, can lead to frustration.

Being a complex phenomenon, frustration could not fetch a clear cut and universally accepted definition. Each psychologist defined it in their own way. Kister defines frustration as a psychological state resulting from the blocking of goal directed activity. According to Coleman, frustration results from the thwarting of a motive either by some obstacles that block or impedes progress toward a desired goal or by the absence of an appropriate goal object. Frustrations may be minor and inconsequential or they may represent serious threats to our welfare or even to our survival.

According to Chauhan and Tiwari, frustrated behaviour lacks goal orientation and appears more or less senseless. Intensity of feelings is there. It is the end of need deprivation. In frustration, a different set of behaviour mechanism is put into operation. For Gilmer (1970), frustration is the state of an organism resulting when the satisfaction of a motivated behaviour is made difficult or impossible, when the way to goal is blocked.

It is noted that all the psychologists agree in their definition one basic principle characteristic of the human behaviour, i.e., all behaviours have motivation or goal direction. All the definitions suggest that frustration is a mental state produced by the motivated behaviour being blocked by some obstacles. It appears more or less senseless. It gets up through need-deprivation. (Govind Tiwari)

VI. Arousal of the Feeling of Frustration

In today's competitive scenario every person has his targets that he wanted to achieve timely and if he is not able to achieve his targets he frustrates. This frustration can affect the mind in negative way in which person's thinking power gets slowed down. Frustration led a person take wrong decision and as a result of which he is not able to come with innovative ideas. His creativity gets stopped down. He is not able to achieve all his targets and is left with only his uncompleted plans and unachieved targets. Such a frustrated person goes far away from reality.

Firstly, the feeling of frustration is aroused in human beings when they are not able to achieve the targets that they had set for themselves. Secondly the feeling of frustration is aroused when they compare themselves with others and find that they are lacking behind while others had made a rapid progress but they had remained where they were earlier. This causes frustration in them when the people misinterpret their capabilities and set those targets which are far away from their potentials. They just compare themselves with those who are more educated or are equipped with high potential or more resources and then set their target up to those levels where they factually could never reach. And then when they are not able to meet their targets they get frustrated.

It is the fact that everyone on this earth is not born with same potential and has same abilities in same area. If they misinterpret their functional area and start career in line in which they are weak or the line which is not meant actually for them; then this results in frustration on the condition of being not achieving the targets.

VII. Causes for Frustration

According to S.K. Mangal, sources of frustration may be physical obstacles such as distance, climate or social phenomenon such as unemployment or lack of friends or they may be internal as lack of physical power, intellectual ability or health. So many people, today, are frustrated because they are not getting enough to feed their children, to give medical treatment to their kith and kin and to provide education and comfort to their families. Frustration is the blocking and un-fulfillment of needs for over a long period of time. Some people fix their ambitions and aspirations too high for their abilities and powers, others have a very high expectation far beyond their actual needs and the cause of frustration is with in them.

But sometimes the source of frustration is outward like unemployment, obstacles, defeat and failures due to political and economic changes over which we have no control.

The cause of frustration may be studied under the major heads, external and internal factors.

(i) *External Factors*

External factors are also called environmental factors. There are the situations or conditions which are present in one's own environment. They affect the individual from outside. The main external factors are as follows:

(a) *Physical Factors:* Natural calamities, obstacles or events in environment also try to block the path of an individual in the attainment of some important goal or the satisfaction of one's basic needs and desires. Even in the physical world such as nail storms, floods, drought, earthquakes, fire accidents, etc., also cause frustration in an individual;

(b) *Social and Societal Factors:* Social forces and social environment may also block the path of an individual either in the attainment of some important goal or in the satisfaction of one's basic needs and desires. In their way, they become the potential source for frustrating motivated individuals. For example: A child may feel frustrated when he is denied permission to go to a movie with his friend, or to a dance or picnic;

(c) *Economic Factors:* Economic and financial factors contribute much in frustrating many individuals. Due to unemployment, young men are inviting death because of frustration. Similarly, many revolts against the social or political set-up witness the results of frustration generated due to severe economic deprivation.

(ii) *Internal Factors*

Internal factors are those which frustrate an individual from within. They are also called personal factors as the person himself is the cause of such frustration.

The main factors in this category are given below:

(a) *Physical Abnormality or Defects:* Too small or too big a stature, very heavy or lean and thin body, an ugly face or dark complexion some glandular or bodily defects such as being equine eyed, blind, deaf or dumb may constitute a source of frustration. Deficiency in one's intelligence or backwardness in a particular subject may also frustrate an individual who is motivated to learn a particular course or choose a particular vocation;

(b) *Conflicting Desires and Aims:* Frustration is also caused by desires and aims;

(c) *Individual's Morality and High Ideals:* An individual's moral standards, code of ethics and high ideals may become a source of frustration to him. He is always caught between his super ego and id. At the same time, when his ego fails to maintain a balance between the two, he becomes frustrated. Due to the weight of the moral standards of his consciences he possesses the unnecessary feeling of guilt or an unusual fear of punishment. For example: He may like to be friendly with a girl but his moral standards do not allow him to do so;

(d) *Level of Aspiration Too High:* One may aspire very high in spite of one's incapabilities or human limitations;

(e) *Lack of Persistence and Sincerity in Efforts:* Frustration may be caused by one's own weaknesses in putting continuous and persistent efforts with courage, enthusiasm and will-power at one's command. One may read a book with no sincere willingness to understand it. After sometime he takes another book and does the same thing with it also. He complains that he is not able to grasp anything after reading too much and thus gives reasons for the feeling of inadequacy that ultimately lead to frustration.

According to Govind Tiwari, often frustrations arise out of psychological barriers in the form of ethical and moral restraints. Frustrations due to biological, psychological and social needs have become very common in this 20th century. Today, we face business, competition, marital problems, social laws and taboos, economic crisis, political competencies, death of loved ones, prejudice, religious dogmas, political dogmas, inadequate self-control, too much responsibilities, etc. which cause frustration.

According to Coleman, primarily, the two sources related to frustration are external (environment) and internal (personal). In the external environmental sources of frustration various physical and social barriers come whereas in the internal sources of frustration arise from the disease, less-intelligence, self-discipline and other psychological causes. The viewpoint of Coleman can be diagrammatically mentioned as below:

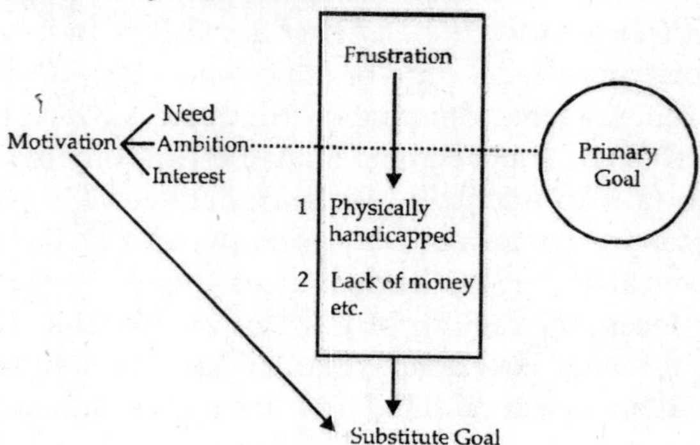

The sources of frustration as such are generally countless. For an easy study they can generally be put into four main categories:

(i) *Man's Physical Environment:* A wide range of environmental obstacles lead to frustration. Inflation, discrimination and death of loved ones are common frustrations stemming from the environment. These external environments create or impose several restrictions that Rosenzweig has called it 'external privation'. They frustrate us in a drastic manner as through heavy rainfall, floods, feminine, draught, earthquake, etc. These unexpected environmental changes obstruct in several ways and ultimately create frustrating situation;

(ii) *Man's Biological Environment:* Man's biological environment is termed by Rosenzweig as 'internal privation'. The biological environment of man—his motor and mental incapabilities are the powerful agents of blocking the motives of individual and resulting into frustration. This type of source of frustration includes personal limitations constitutional defects which later on develops feelings of insecurity and lackness in personal worth which later on results in frustration;

(iii) *Man's Social Environment:* The Social milieu is the significant source of frustration. The social set-up, social norms, taboos, prejudices, cultural-cum-religious norms, etc., play an important role in satisfying the needs. The present economic system is rigid and man cannot fulfill even his basic needs of life because acquisition of money is a difficult task. The economic power is not equally distributed. This is the position of almost all the countries of the world. Those who are financially well equipped, tend to control the society as well as the nation through their economic power. By doing so, they perplex in the state of frustration. In contrary, those who are economically deprived are struggling to fulfill the basic needs of their family. In striving, they involve in frustrated situation. Horney (1945) found social milieu as a significant source in frustration causing neurosis;

(iv) *Man's Psychological Environment:* Man is complex by nature. He is not a subject who gives one response at a time to a stimulus. He has a number of simultaneous, overlapping psychological situations which make him remarkably complex. This is quite possible for several needs and demands to arise at the same time in him but due to disruptive of other he cannot fulfill all of them. This creates a tenseful situation or conflict in him which is the strongest source of frustration. Ruch (1970) quotes that when an individual is compelled to choose one or the other of the two goals or has both positive and negative feelings about a particular goal, he faces conflict and frustration. Sanford (1961) writes it as 'the state of being simultaneously motivated by incompatible mutually exclusive tendencies, when the individual is placed under tension through the arousal of two or more opposing motives within himself, he is in a state of conflict'. We can conceive some of the conflicting motivational tendencies being aroused by two equally attractive or equally repulsive objects in environment.

According to Ramnath Sharma, working knowledge of the nature and consequences of frustration need to be known. It is now possible to pursue analysing its sources or causes (Sharma) of which the main are the following:

(i) *Aiming Beyond One's Abilities:* As has been pointed out for achieving success, it is essential that the individual's objective should be within his power and capacity. Many people pose before themselves objectives that have no regard of their actual capability and are outside their reach. As a consequence, their life becomes a tale of frustration and woe, and they always appear disconsolate, anxious, irritable and disturbed. Here, it is necessary to understand that psychologically every individual cannot be made into anything. Hence, an individual should take care to select an objective and aim that is within his power, and having done so, should exert himself to the very utmost;

(ii) *Lack of Requisite Effort:* When frustration meets some effort of ours, it should not be taken for granted that it is outside our power, since the failure may be either due to lack of necessary effort or due to a wrong approach and defective methodology. These difficulties can be overcome with ease;

(iii) *Competition:* Frustration would have been an unknown phenomenon in human life, as every pleasure and all the good things of life had been freely available, as are water and air. But this is not the condition with regard to most physical amenities. There are very many things and traits such as wealth, money, property, beauty, attractive personality, high character, fame, etc., in which there is not enough of it to go round, as the saying is. The desire to possess them is present in every individual, and acute-throat competition exists between men for them. In this unequal struggle, frustration and failure come to many and bliss only to a very few;

(iv) *Social and Cultural Obstacles:* Another very fundamental cause of frustration consists in the taboos inflicted by society and culture upon the expression of our motives. In his book Civilisation and its Discontents', Freud, the famous psychoanalyst, has shown how man has had to play the price of civilisation in terms of frustration and mental agony. And among the various social and cultural taboos the most effective and the most powerful is the one concerned with sex impulse and its expression; and Freud has indulged in a detailed consideration of the mental aberrations and abnormalities resultant upon such restraint. Anthropologists have found that fewer frustrations are to be seen in the population of ancient tribal people in which social and cultural taboos are fewer than in the allegedly more civilised societies;

(v) *Physical Cause:* Man exists in a physical environment upon the machinations of which he has little control; hence such physical phenomena and events as flood, plague, earthquake, excessive rain, drought, etc., are some of the sources of frustration in man;

(vi) *Political Cause:* Every human individual is part and parcel of a political organisation, and the manifestation of many of his instincts is controlled and limited by the state. Hence, the result of this control is evident in the frustration of numerous motives that would otherwise have been satisfied.

Frustrations arising from the above sources may be simple just as much as they may be complex. Simple frustrations are very much a part of every one's life and are often a spur to one's activity since they increase our enthusiasm to achieve some end that is eluding us, but the arising of the complex frustrations can lead to a person becoming tendentious towards abnormality and mental disease. Such states and calamities may be avoided if one tries to keep a sane and healthy outlook on these frustrations. And the first step towards such a healthy and sane outlook is the clear realisation that frustration is a natural and inevitable part of human life. Many thinkers have gone so far as to opine that frustration is essential if success is to be attained and prosperity is to be achieved. Secondly, when a frustration thrusts itself on one's mind one should consider it with a cool mind, analyse its causes, and make an effort to get rid of them. In this manner, one may evade the evil consequences of frustration and secure adjustment with his circumstances. (Ramnath Sharma)

According to S. Dandapani:

1. Environmental forces that block motive fulfillments as diagrammed beside:

Barrier and Frustration

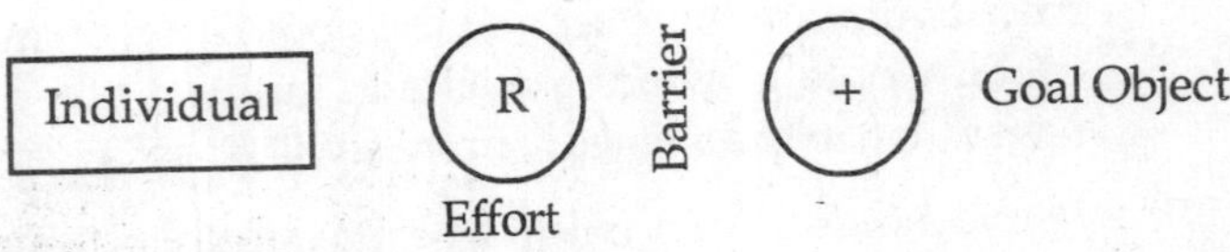

2. Personal limitations that block motive fulfillment;
3. Conflict of motives can cause frustration.

According to D.N. Srivastava, The reactions of organism mainly depend on two things: 1. Strength of motivation; and 2. Distance from goal: The degree of frustration in the person also depends upon these two things. Description of general sources producing frustration is given below:

1. *Competition:* As social being, the facilities and sources man gets are not equal for all people and persons. Most of the persons in the society struggle complete hard to equalise their prestige, standard, etc., with others. In this race of competition, a person moves forward and the other is left behind; the person left behind when feels himself unsuccessful and unable to overcome the obstacles, then he is frustrated in their situation. A person when expects success and meets failure, he develops frustration;

2. *High Level of Aspiration:* When the level of aspiration is high in a person than his abilities, he expects success is many fields. But because of his inabilities he receives failure usually, such situation generates frustration. In the absence of proper abilities and with high level of aspiration, a person has to bear many punishments and loss, this situation too produces frustration;

3. *Inborn Disabilities:* Some inborn inabilities like blindness, deafness, stammering, any serious untreatable disease, etc., or inabilities developed after birth, the person feels himself inferior to others in his race of life. It is natural that person meets failure when he starts the work with inferiority complex. Inferiority feeling and failure produces frustration in the person;

4. *External Factors:* The above given three factors are internal factors. Some of the external factors described here also naturally produce frustration: (a) Natural Environmental Factors—Factors earthquake, flood, disaster, fire etc. are such serious problems, which are likely to produce frustration; (b) Accidents—Various accidents also make the person economically, physically, and mentally weak, and in this state of weakness the person becomes helpless

to overcome the obstacles and then frustration becomes obvious; (c) Political Causes; (d) Social Obstacles - Social obstacles are also good sources of frustration.

According to P. Yakaiah and K.K. Bhatia, human psyche is the seat of both mutually exclusive and mutually inclusive happenings. It is here that passions rise, leading some time to elation and another time to depression, fear, anxiety, anger and even sense of quite. The goal is ahead; behaviour is directed towards the goal, blockage in the way thwarts success and develops frustration. Thus, the term frustration refers to the blocking of behaviour directed towards a goal. The term may also refer to an event or the consequence of an event. 'A frustrating event is one in which goal-directed activity is blocked, slowed up or otherwise interferred with'. When it refers to 'a consequence of blocked goal-seeking', confusion and annoyance may leave a man in frustration. So, frustration may turn out to be a state of unpleasant emotional outburst.

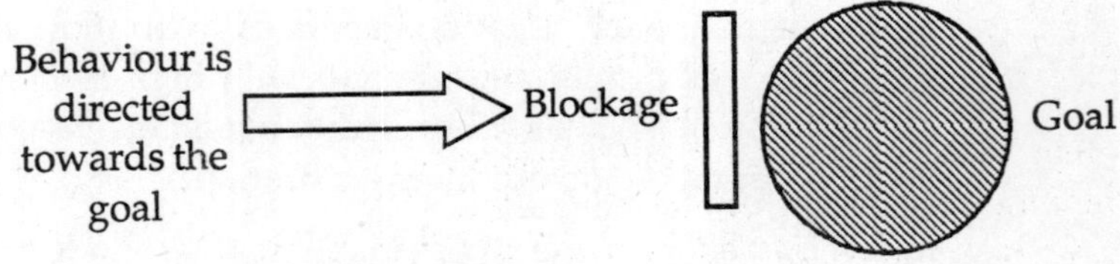

According to Morgan and his associates, there may be 3 causes of frustration:

(i) *Forces in the Environment:* Sometimes, forces in the environment block the fulfillment of motives. This leads to frustration. An obstacle may be something physical such as closing of the office, a locked door, non-availability of funds, etc., or it may be people—parents, teachers, employers, or police officers. In either of the above cases, fulfillment of the goal may be blocked;

(ii) *Personal Weaknesses:* Sometimes, an individual may set his eye on a certain goal which is beyond his ability to achieve. People are often frustrated because they are compelled to aspire for unattainable goals. A parent may wish their mediocre son to become an IAS officer. His performance will remain far short of the required level. Both the parents and the child will suffer from frustration;

(iii) *Conflict as Cause of Frustration:* Conflict among motives may become the cause of frustration. If the expression of one motive interferes with the expression of another motive, the result is frustration.

Frustration and Anger

We all have experienced irritation and anger at some frustrations. A long line preventing us from seeing an eagerly awaited movie, a crush of shoppers hindering the purchase of some simple necessities, a slow driver obstructing a narrow road, probably have aroused in all of us that familiar flush of annoyance, even anger. That frustration of our desires and goals occasionally leads to anger in a common place. It is subjectively unquestionable—a fact of our existence.

Of course, not all frustrations lead to anger. Indeed, it is more common to accept frustration the blockage of our wants or goals as feedback suggesting what we adjust or alter our aims. We do this automatically, hour by hour, day by day. Frustration signals the error in the trial-and-error process by which we dialectically adjust our perspectives to external powers and potentialities. To live, to assert oneself, is to be hindered, to face difficulties, to be opposed. Noise in the background; my desire for physical comfort is defeated by the summer heat; my search for the right words to express my 'understanding' is blocked by the barrier between structured language and unstructured 'insight' and feelings. Moreover, when I let my consciousness stroll through the nested levels of my existence, I am also aware of a multitude of frustrations that reach consciousness like a flock of pheasants startled out of tall grass. Frustrations associated with family, research, teaching, politics, and the growing structure of coercive rules and laws. As I write, my life is within a matrix of such frustrations, high and low, large and small, significant and trivial.

Yet, at the moment, I am at the content, relatively happy, and feel no irritation, no anger.

Frustration and Aggression

Aggression is always a consequence of frustration. More specifically the proposition is that the occurrence of aggressive behaviour always presupposes the existence of frustration and, contrariwise, that the existence of frustration always leads to some form of aggression.

The widespread acceptance of the frustration-aggression notion is perhaps attributable more to its simplicity than to its predictive power. In a point of fact, the formula that frustration breeds aggression does not hold up well under empirical scrutiny in laboratory studies in which conditions regarded as frustrative are systematically varied... Frustration, as commonly defined, is only one and not necessarily the most important factor affecting the expression of aggression. (Bandura, 1973)

The primary source of the human capacity for violence appears to be the frustration-aggression mechanism. Frustration does not necessarily lead to violence, and violence for some men is motivated by expectations of gain. The anger induced by frustration, however, is a motivating force that disposes men to aggression, irrespective of its instrumentalities. If frustrations are sufficiently prolonged or sharply felt, aggression is quite likely, if not certain, to occur. To conclude that the relationship is not relevant to individual or collective violence is akin to the assertion that the law of gravitation is irrelevant to the theory of flight because not everything that goes up falls back to earth in accord with the basic gravitational principle. The frustration-aggression mechanism is in this sense analogous to the law of gravity: men who are frustrated have an innate disposition to do violence to its source in proportion to the intensity of their frustrations . . . (Gurr, 1970).

Poor Management in Organisations

Frustration can be a result of blocking motivated bahaviour. An individual may react in several different ways. He may respond with rational problem-solving methods to overcome the barrier. Failing in this, he may become frustrated and behave irrationally. An example of blockage of motivational energy would be the case of the worker who wants time off to go fishing but is denied permission by his supervisor. Another example would be the executive who wants a promotion but finds he lacks certain qualifications. If, in these cases, an appeal to reason does not succeed in reducing the barrier or in developing some reasonable alternative approach, the frustrated individual may resort to less adaptive methods of trying to reach his goal. He may, for example, attack the barrier physically or verbally or both. The worker who is refused time off to go fishing may 'cuss out' his supervisor to his face or behind his back. If he is sufficiently aroused, he may strike out at him with his fists or with the nearest weapon. If the supervisor is not present or the worker's fear of the consequences of direct attack is stronger than his desire to attack, he may transfer his aggression to someone or something else. Taking his frustration out on his family or on some object like his car or his equipment are typical ways of transferring aggression.

Another solution to frustration is regressive bahaviour—becoming childish or reverting to earlier and more primitive ways of coping with the goal barrier. Throwing a temper tantrum, bursting into tears, or sulking are examples of regression. Wearing a long face and a worried look are other signs of this method of dealing with frustration.

Stubborn refusal to respond to new conditions affecting the goal, such as removal or modification of the barrier, sometimes occurs. As pointed out by Brown, severe punishment may cause individuals to continue non-adaptive behaviour blindly.

Either it may have an effect opposite to that of reward and as such, discourage the repetition of the act, or, by functioning as a frustrating agent, it may lead to fixation and the other symptoms of frustration as well. It follows that punishment is a dangerous tool, since it often has effects which are entirely the opposite of those desired. (Brown)

An example of non-adaptive behaviour of this sort might occur in case of the executive who feels persecuted by his failure to be promoted. Even when offered a training course to improve his chances of promotion, he turns down this opportunity and continues to sulk.

Flight, or leaving the scene, is another way people have dealing with their frustrations. In the above example of the executive, we might find him quitting his job rather than face up to the consequences of being passed over for promotion. Or, a player quits the football squad because he is not given enough playing time or fails to win the starting berth as quarterback.

Managers must learn to recognise the symptoms of frustration to avoid responding in ways that intensify rather than ameliorate the problem. The main point to remember is that the affected person is often not in a rational, problem-solving frame of mind and is, therefore, not attuned to the 'facts' or to logical procedures for dealing with his situation. Some frustrated people need to be guided back to 'reality'. They cannot be reasoned within their present mental state. Listening with understanding to such a person is one effective way to reduce frustration. Talking to a sympathetic listener provides a way for him to vent his feelings and regain control of himself.

Motives provide energy and direction for behaviour. Appropriate bahaviour, in turn, reduces the inner tensions that signal the motivated state. An understanding of the relationships among motives, bahaviour, and human goals provides the manager, administrator, or leader with a way of thinking about human activity and a framework within which to gather, sort, and analyse data related to behavioural problems.

VIII. The Stresses of Care-giving

Suffering seems to be one of those fundamental human experiences that we all have in common, and is perhaps the one we would all gladly give up. We often feel oppressed and frustrated by suffering because we do not understand it. It can pierce the heart of our being and our identity, and shake every assumption we hold about ourselves and the world. It often seems to destroy our will-power and overthrow our commitments, to our dismay:

1. Frustration is a normal and valid emotional response to many of the difficulties of being a caregiver. While some irritation may be part of everyday life as a caregiver, feeling extreme frustration can have serious consequences for you or the person you care for. Frustration and stress may negatively impact your physical health or cause you to be physically or verbally aggressive towards your loved

one. If your care-giving situation is causing you extreme frustration or anger, you may want to explore some new techniques for coping;

2. Caring for an individual with Alzheimer's disease or a related dementia can be challenging and, at times, overwhelming;

3. Frustration often arises out of trying to change an uncontrollable circumstance. As a caregiver of someone with dementia, you face many uncontrollable situations. Normal daily activities—dressing, bathing and eating may become sources of deep frustration for you.

IX. Warning Signs of Frustration

Warning signs of frustration can be intervened and adjust the mood before losing control. Some of the common warning signs of frustration include:

1. Shortness of breath
2. Knot in the throat
3. Stomach cramps
4. Chest pains
5. Headache
6. Compulsive eating
7. Excessive alcohol consumption
8. Increased smoking
9. Lack of patience
10. Desire to strike out

X. Reactions of Frustrations

According to Govind Tiwari, frustration creates a tenseful situation or uncomfortable emotional condition which ultimately encourages the individual to engage in various tension reducing activities. Technically, this is called 'reaction to frustration'. The variety of reactions to frustration is unlimited because every individual adopts his own way to reduce his tensions. According to

Page: 'The reactions may range from the constructive direct approaches of normal individuals to the mental symptoms of psychotic patients'. The main reactions to frustration (Tiwari) are given below:

1. *Direct Reactions Toward Frustrations*

When one fails to achieve the desired goal, then primarily he uses two methods of removing obstacles through the increased effort and variation in mode of attack. These two methods are discussed below:

(a) *Increased trails and change in methods:* When an individual fails to achieve a goal, then he increases his trials or adopts other means to reach the goal;

(b) *Change in goal:* If the individual fails to remove his frustration by increasing the trails or changing the methods, then he ultimately changes his goal. The change of goal occurs in two forms—either selection of lesser intensity of goal (determining the goal to II class instead of I class) or accept the other goal (for example, a science student changes his subject to arts and selects home science, education etc.).

2. *Indirect Reaction Toward Frustrations*

When an individual fails to get over the frustrations through direct reactions, he adopts indirect means of reactions. These indirect reactions toward frustration are given below:

(a) *Inferiority Complex:* Individuals who think that there is any defect in their personality and as such they might not attain their objectives, develop inferiority complex within. They appear to be suspicious, worried, introvert type and always fearing the competitions. It is noteworthy that idiots never suffer from their complexity. They remain alike in failure whereas intellectuals can not even face minor failure and develop inferiority complex within them. It is quite possible to remove their complexity from the personality. Mainly two methods are adopted for the treatment as: (i) Determination of an individual's objective on the basis of his capabilities; (ii) By removing the personality defects and emphasising more attempts. The inferiority complex has its own merits. Sometimes an individual on account of his inferiority complex increases his efforts and achieves success. For example, Roosevelt was very weak in childhood. He was much worried about his physical weakness. Through his continuous efforts, he was able to overcome his physical weakness. But on the other hand sometimes due to inferiority complex individuals develop within themselves several mental diseases;

(b) *Aggressive Behaviour:* An individual's reaction to failures is often displayed in his aggressive behaviour. There may be direct or indirect or both that forms or form aggressive behaviour. Sometimes, the person himself becomes the object of his aggressive behaviour as beating his own head whereas sometimes other people are the object of aggressive behaviour. We find several examples of this behaviour in our daily life. If a child's wish is not fulfilled, then sometimes he expresses his aggressive behaviour directly while sometimes through negligence. The aggressive behaviour is besides being harmful to the individual himself, harms others as well;

(c) *Mental Mechanism:* Sometimes the reactions of conflicts, failures or inferiority complex are in the form of 'mental mechanism'. Actually, mental mechanism is the best possible solution of reaction of failures. According to McDowell, 'mental mechanisms are reactions by which the frustrated instincts obtain satisfaction in an oblique way which is acceptable to the community'. Due to failures or maladjustment, an individual stably or unstably arises at a tenseful situation and through mental mechanism tries to get some satisfaction. Some prominent mental mechanisms are fantasy, compensation, identification, projection, rationalisation and sublimation.

According to Ramnath Sharma, the reactions for frustration are as follows:

1. *Creation of or Increase in Emotional Tension:* A child is naturally and very strongly motivated and inclined to go out of the house and to play with other children of his own age. If he is prevented from doing so, he evinces definite signs of labouring under great emotional tension, and this tension remains till the frustrated emotion succeeds in finding some mode of release. And this expression can take the normal form or instead it can be manifested through different kinds of mental mechanisms;

2. *Increase in Effort:* A healthy person's reaction to frustration is in the form of increased efforts towards overcoming the obstacle causing the frustration. Actually, when frustration fails to a person's lot in life, then he should think upon the causes of that frustration, since it is not essential that failure is inevitably the outcome of a low degree of enterprise in the individual. It is possible that the work he is trying to perform is outside of his capability, as not many students succeed in studying a subject that interests them not. But if the failure to attain a goal is the result of our lack of effort or enterprise, then the best one can do is to step up the effort, in complete disregard of the frustration suffered;

3. *Different Approach:* Another cause that often dogs our foot-steps in life is the choice of a wrong method of approach. If frustration is the outcome of such faulty orientation, then success can be had for the asking in the future by changing one's method of approach, and quite a number of people intuitively realise their fact. When a sensible man fails to attain his objective through one approach, he immediately tries another, and in their manner sticks to trial and error till he discovers the one correct method of action;

4. *Change of Objective:* On the other hand, when some people fail to obtain their object, they avoid frustration in this line by changing their very goal. And the goal can be changed in the following ways: first by reducing the objective and aiming at a lower level, and second by entirely adopting a different goal;

5. *Sense of Inferiority:* All the reactions to frustration mentioned so far are simple and straight forward, and may be seen in a large majority of individuals but there are certain other reactions that are more indicative of abnormal behaviour. For example, when frustration meets certain people they not only refuse to change their method but also their aim. In other words, they do not accommodate themselves, and instead, get into the habit of regarding them as very weak, helpless and unfortunate. A tense mental state of this kind is called the sense of inferiority. A person full of the sense of inferiority looks only to his own shortcomings and is always afraid of intuiting criticism from and disregard of others. Mental characteristics such as suspicious, jealousy, criticism of others, anxiety, introvert tendencies, fear of competition, high emotional excitability towards criticism, very profound reactions to failure, etc., are to be seen in his life. This sense of inferiority is not caused by actual deficiency of interests and abilities in the individual. It has instead been seen that many unintelligent students do not allow this sense of inferiority even on the slightest failure. Thus, the sense of inferiority is a concomitant not of a capacity but of character. Very highly ambitious people have very many frustrations and thus their sense of inferiority, once it is developed, is also strong. Consequently, it can be reasoned that in order to avoid the sense of inferiority away from him an individual should first of all try to aim at something that is within his own capabilities to achieve, and secondly, he should spare no effort to attain this end. There is a proverb: know what you can do and do it like a Hercules;

6. *Aggressive Behaviour:* Often, the reaction to frustration takes the form of aggressive behaviour. It is proverbially said that the bad worker blames his tools since he wants to transfer the blame for his failure to the tools. It is observed commonly that when people are scolded in office for their inefficient work, they work off their steam and charge by being angry with the children at home

when in a aggressive mood, sparked off by frustration, an individual can, directly or indirectly, launch an attack on others, but in quite a large majority of people this worth turns in upon themselves rather than on other people or objects. They take to beating their hands with their hands or banging it into the nearest handy wall, while the more disturbed go to the extreme of committing suicide. It goes without saying that those who commit suicide after leaving some note accusing someone give a blow to him more severe than direct physical assault. It is because of this close intimacy between frustration and aggressive behaviour which has been observed that some psychologists have cited frustration as an important cause of war, and they have further suggested that if wars are to be eliminated from human society, then such conditions be created in which frustrations of every field of life be at their minimum possible. The most dangerous forms of aggressive behaviour are the consequences of sex frustration. Such a fact is borne out if we study the life histories of notorious master criminals;

7. *Mental Mechanisms:* Sometimes, the reaction to frustration is evident in the form of mental mechanisms, the main ones being fantasy, compensation, identification, projection, sublimation and rationalisation

According to D.N. Srivastava, aggression, compromise and withdrawal are the modes or reactions of frustration.

Fisher, V.E. (1952) states that by the above three methods of responding, clear knowledge of the frustrated person's mental status and process is not possible. Therefore, he gives following responding methods: viz., adjustment reactions, practically adjustment reactions, non- adjustment reactions and maladjustment reactions.

The relation of above methods of response given by Fisher for frustration is with therapeutic and abnormal psychology. A description of the reaction to frustration on which experimental work is done is given below. Most of the psychologists agree with these methods of reaction to frustration.

These responses are as follows:

Frustration — Aggressive Hypothesis

Frustration — Regression Hypothesis

Frustration — Fixation Hypothesis

According to S.K. Mangal, the following are the reactions of frustration:

1. ***Simple Reactions***

Under these reactions we may include the following :

(a) *Increasing trials or improving efforts:* During the period of frustration, some individuals go through introspection and for overcoming the obstacles either increase their efforts or bring about improvement in their behaviour or processes;

(b) *Adopting compromising means:* Repeated failure in one direction may lead the individual to change the direction of his efforts. For example, an aspirant for I.A.S. may, after his failure, direct his energies to pass the provincial civil service examination. A girl's mother failing to marry her daughter to a handsome boy may be contented by a tolerable complexion;

(c) *Withdrawal:* The individual learns to move away from the situation that causes him frustration. A child withdraws himself from the game that he does not know. A Youngman may refuse to marry because of his sexual incompetence;

(d) *Submissiveness:* Here the individual surrenders himself and accepts his defeat before the conditions causing frustration. A child may become much submissive after failing in his attempts in some direction.

2. ***Violent Reactions***

In addition to the above mentioned simple reactions the individual becomes emotionally tense and resorts to aggressive activities. This aggression is of two types—external and internal.

(a) *External Aggression:* "This aggression", as Carroll observes, "may be directed towards either the person or persons who caused the frustration or towards the substitute or substitutes". A clerk in his frustration of not getting promotion may quarrel with his officer or rebuke his wife or beat his children. A boy experiencing frustration in the playground may try to hit the boy denying him the chance of carrying the ball or may use his younger brother or parents as substitute for releasing his tension;

(b) *Internal aggression:* It is an aggression turned towards the self. Instead of releasing one's emotional tensions by attacking others, one resorts to the attack of one's self. Instead of blaming others, the individual blames himself. Although self criticism does not do any harm, but the excessive aggression towards the self is destructive for the self. Eventually, the person becomes neurotic or tries to find escape through suicide. As far as the well-being of the individual is concerned this inward aggression is far more dangerous than outward aggression.

XI. Ways to Handle Frustration or Remedies of Frustration

Everyone, who has any goals, experiences frustration and disappointment. Without goals or challenges, one may live an empty life.

All of us experience tragedies and disappointments which sometimes have nothing to do with us. Bad stuff just happens sometimes. Most people get depressed or frustrated a few times a month. It feels like "Everything and everyone stinks! I stink! Nothing will ever work out for me".

1. Healthy Ways and Unhealthy Ways

A list of healthy ways, unhealthy ways and questionable ways to handle frustration are detailed hereunder:

Healthy Ways	*Unhealthy Ways*	*Questionable Ways*
Taking to someone you trust	Trying to hurt your self	Eating something
Listening to or creating music or creating art	Trying to hurt someone else being a bulky	Spending money
Playing a sport or doing exercise	Smoking	Working
Doing something you like	Drinking or chugging	Body piercing
Taking a nap	Kicking the cat or some other animal.	
Meditating	Gambling	
Thinking about what went wrong and trying to do better next time	Unhealthy sex	

2. Calming Down Physically

When you become aware of the warning signs of frustration, you can intervene with an immediate activity to help you calm down. This gives you time to look at the situation more objectively and to choose how to respond in a more controlled way. When you feel yourself becoming frustrated, try counting from one to ten slowly and take a few deep breaths. If you are able take a brief walk or go to another room and collect your thoughts. It is better to leave the situation, even for a moment, than to lose control or react in a way you will regret. If you think someone may be offended when you leave the room, you can tell that person you need to go to the restroom. You can also try calling a friend, praying, meditation, singing, listening to music or taking a bath. Try experimenting with different responses to find out what works best for you and the person you care for.

3. Relaxation Techniques

The regular practice of relaxation techniques can also help prepare for frustrating circumstance. If possible, try the following relaxation exercise for at least ten minutes each day! Sit in a comfortable position in a quiet place. Take slow, deep breath and relax the tension in your body. While you continue to take slow and deep breaths, you may want to imagine a safe and restful place and repeat a claming word or phrase.

4. Communicating Assertively

Good communication can reduce frustration by allowing you to express yourself while helping others to understand your limits and needs. Assertive communication is different from passive or aggressive communication. When you communicate passively, you may be keeping your own needs and desires inside to avoid conflict with others. While this may seem easier on the surface, the long term result may be that others feel they can push you around to get their way.

When you communicate aggressively, you may be forcing your needs and desires onto others. While this allows you to express your feelings, aggressive communication generally makes others more defensive and less cooperative.

When you communicate assertively, you express your own needs and desires while respecting the needs and desires of others. Assertive communication allows both parties to engage in a dignified discussion about the issue at hand. Keys to assertive communication are: (1) Respecting your own feelings, needs and desires; (2) Standing up for your feelings without shaming, degrading or humiliating the other person; (3) Using "I" statements rather than "you" statements. (4) Not using "should" statements.

5. The Critical Step: Asking for Help

(1)Accepting the need of help and asking for help will ultimately reduce frustration; (2) You can not take on all the responsibilities of care giving by yourself; (3) Discuss your needs with family members and friends who might be willing to share care giving responsibilities. People will not realize you need help if you do not explain your situation and ask for assistance; (4) Remember, you have the right to ask for help and express your needs.

6. Self-care to Prevent Frustration

Care-giving can be tiring and stressful when you're caring for others, it's easy to forget to care for yourself. While it may be difficult to find time to focus on yourself and your needs, it is very important that you do so to prevent frustration and burnout.

7. Make Time for Yourself

You may feel guilty about needing or wanting time for our rest, socialisation and fun. However, everyone deserves regular and ongoing breaks from work, including caregivers. 'Respite' providers can give you the opportunity to take the breaks you need. Respite breaks may be provided by in-home help, adult day care, 'friendly visitor' programmes, friends and neighbours, or other means. The important point it is to allow yourself to take a break from care giving. Required periodical rest and relaxation will help you keeping out of frustration several times and situations.

8. Take care of yourself

Although care giving may make it difficult to find time for yourself, it is important to eat well, exercise, get a night's good sleep and attend to your own medical needs. When you do not take care of yourself, you are prone to increased anxiety, depression, frustration and physical distress that will make it more difficult to continue providing care.

9. Seek Outside Support

Sharing your feelings with a counsellor, a support group, or with another caregiver in a similar situation can be a great way to release stress and get helpful advice.

10. Precautions to Prevent Frustration

To conclude:

- Learn to recognise the warning signs of frustration;
- Intervene to calm yourself down physically;
- Modify your thoughts in a way that reduces your stress;
- Learn to communicate assertively;
- Learn to ask for help.

RESEARCH STUDIES

The researcher has traced a few researches done in the past on the subject of frustration and the findings of those researches were cited hereunder for working in a better way with the present study on the frustration of prospective teachers.

1. Frustration and Gender

Srivastava, P. K. (1980) stated that the male and female lecturers did not differ significantly on the measure of teaching efficiency whereas the males exhibited greater amount of frustration than the females.

Malviya, I. (1968) reported that the frustration reactions of the male and female subjects were found to be differed. The mean score was higher on reactions of males than that of females. Males were also more aggressive than females.

Mithal, S. L. (1975) found that the frustrated boys were predominantly extra-aggressive while the girls were ingressive; the difference between the boys and the girls behaviour was significantly different this was true of boys and girls of graduate level also.

Gyanoni, T. C. (1984) reported that boys with high achievement motivation were intropunitive and need persistent, but low in extrapunitive and 'O-D' behaviour. The boys with a low level of achievement motivation were found to be more ego-defensive, obstacle dominant and impunitive in their behaviour.

Sharma, U. (1985) found that working women with high socio-economic status were optimistic of getting over a frustrating obstacle, whereas those with low socio-economic status tried to avoid it or deny its presence and to blame others.

Goyal, Chhaya (1988) reported that drive was a significant determinant of learning and speed of performance in college-going female adolescents.

Sharma, Suman (1988) reported that sex did not affect attitudes and frustration level.

Gupta, Deoyani (1990) reported that both boys and girls had incidence of frustration to a considerable extent; and girls were significantly more frustrated than boys.

Biswas, P. C. (1989) found that sex had little differential effect on frustration reaction patterns.

Shandilya, Manorama (1990) reported that male teachers of central schools showed a relationship between frustration, age, service conditions and work-load. Female teachers of central schools indicated no relationship between frustration and emolument, age, service conditions and work-load. Male and female teachers of state government schools indicated a relationship between work-load and frustration. Male teachers of private schools showed a relationship between frustration and service conditions. No relationship existed between frustration and other variables, i.e., emoluments, age and work-load. While female teachers of private schools showed a relationship between frustration and emoluments and frustration service conditions.

2. Frustration and Locality

Sharma, Suman (1988) observed that residential area had no effect on attitudes and frustration.

Biswas, P. C. (1989) found that whereas rural, urban and school climate had little differential effect on frustration reaction patterns.

3. Frustration and Age

Shandilya, Manorama (1990) reported that age and service conditions showed no relationship with frustration; and no relationship existed between frustration and age and frustration and work-load.

Biswas, P. C. (1989) found that age had a significant differential effect on frustration reaction patterns.

Gyanoni, T. C. (1984) reported that at all age groups the percentage of E and E-D reactions was comparatively in relation to other frustration reactions; ego defensive and obstacle dominate reactions to frustration decreased as the subjects advanced in age but their need-persistent reactions significantly increased with increase in their age; and a significant increase in intropunitive behaviour was observed, whereas impunitive frustration reaction increased with age but a significant fall in this particular reaction was observed after the age of 20 years.

Srivastava, P. K. (1980) found no linear relationship between the frustration and the teaching efficiency of teachers of various age groups.

4. Frustration and Motivation

Dubey, P. (1980) found that in the condition of frustration the levels of motivation decreased and at particular stage of frustration individuals left the game; and frustration become the cause for another motivation for the next drive to achieve success.

5. Frustration and Conflict

Dubey, P. (1980) found that the frustrated individuals were more affected by suggestions, and suggestions also helped them in decreasing the degree of conflict, and the frustrated individuals took more time than the successful group to select an alternative for their drive to draw wooden squares, and a high degree of conflict existed between frustrated and successful individuals.

6. Frustration and Attitude

Dubey, P. (1980) found that the frustrated individuals formed aggressive and other reactions against the game, the observer, judgement and the winners. A negative attitude was formed in the frustrated individuals.

7. Frustration and Maladjustment

Verma (1968) noticed that frustration and maladjustment in retarded school adolescents.

8. Frustration and Adjustment

Goyal, Chhaya (1988) reported that interaction between different areas of adjustment and different modes of frustration was significant, except in the case of aggression and emotional adjustment; and adjustment and frustration interacted among themselves while affecting learning and speed of performance of female adolescents.

Gupta, Deoyani (1990) stated that a significant and negative correlation was found between frustration and adjustment, intelligence and academic achievement.

9. Frustration and Teaching Efficiency

Srivastava, P. K. (1980) reported that: (1) frustration induced through the various techniques adversely affected the teaching efficiency of the student-teachers; (2) Frustration induced through suspension, charge-sheet and detention adversely affected the teaching of the fixative and regressive group, where as in case of the aggressive group of student-teachers it had an inverse effect on their teaching efficiency. Similarly, verbal warning had an adverse effect on the teaching efficiency of the aggressively and regressively frustrated group of student-teachers, whereas it had an inverse effect on the fixative frustrated group; (3) The lecturers belonging to the high educational attainment group scored significantly higher than those belonging to the low educational attainment group on the measures of teaching efficiency and frustration whereas on these two measures the lecturers with longer or shorter teaching experience as well as those drawing larger or smaller emoluments did not differ significantly; (4) The older lecturers expressed relatively greater amount of frustration and inferior teaching efficiency than the younger lecturers; (5) The male and female lecturers did not differ significantly on the measure of teaching efficiency whereas the males exhibited greater amount of frustration than the females; (6) Frustration and teaching efficiency had a low positive relationship; (7) There existed a very low positive relationship between the measures of frustration and teaching efficiency of various groups having different lengths of teaching experience. This relationship was linear and went on deteriorating as the teaching experience advanced; (8) There existed no linear relationship between the frustration and the teaching efficiency of teachers of various age groups.

10. Frustration and Reactions

Malviya, I. (1968) reported that: (1) The frustration reactions of the male and female subjects were found to be differed. The mean score was higher on reactions of males than of females. Males were also more aggressive than females; (2) The reaction pattern of adolescents and adults was different; (3) Inward threat and passive threat responses were lower in adolescents while on outward problems and inward problems adolescents showed higher mean scores; (4) The score for aggressive responses was higher in the rural group, though the difference was not significant; (5) Aggressive responses of the non-Hindu group were a little higher than those of Hindu group; (6) The urban adolescent males were more problem-solving than rural adolescent males; (7) The non-Hindu adult males were considerably more aggressive than Hindu adult males; (8) The comparison between higher-lower economic statuses was more significant than the other two; (9) The reaction to frustration was found to be affected by high scores on neuroticism and extroversion. (10) The subjects were found to be different in their reactions under actual and ideal conditions.

11. Frustration and Mental Health

Bhattacharjee, M. (1985) reported that: (1) There was a high positive correlation between frustration and mental ill health; (2) The less the frustration of idealistic and altruistic need the more the mental ill health and vice versa; (3) Incidence of mental ill-health was high; (4) There was a negative relationship between mental ill-health and frustration-intoleration of the idealistic and altruistic need.

12. Frustration and Frustration Intoleration

Bhattacharjee, M. (1985) reported that: (1) The needs, frustration, frustration-intoleration and mental health of adolescent girls reading in certain urban secondary schools; (2) Extent of frustration-intoleration of these five needs was high; (3) Materialistic sexual relationship, security and independence needs were high. Not only was this, but the extent of frustration with regard to these needs also high; (4) There was a high positive correlation between frustration and frustration-intoleration and mental health; (5) There was a negative relationship between mental ill-health and frustration-intoleration of the idealistic and altruistic need.

13. Frustration and Anxiety

Gyanoni, T.C. (1984) reported that the students with a high level of anxiety were found to be more intropunitive and obstacle, dominant, whereas the low level anxiety boys were more impunitive and need persistent.

Jethwani, P. M. (1980) found that the pupils having high anxiety were significantly more frustrated than the pupils having less anxiety.

14. Frustration and Drive

Goyal, Chhaya (1988) reported that interaction between drive and significant modes of frustration was not significant; and interaction between drive and different areas of adjustment was not significant.

15. Frustration and Economic Conditions

Tohsin (1978) found that economic conditions also resulted in frustration. The other problematic areas were health, physical growth, finance, living conditions, sex, employment, home, family, etc.

16. Frustration and Retention

Mahadik, Arun Kumar (1988) reported that (1) Experimentally induced frustration considerably hampered retention, but the existing level of frustration did not significantly affect relation. (2) The joint effect of value-orientation and induced frustration did not yield significant effect, but the effect of the frustration treatment on retention with respect to type and degree of value-orientation was found significant. (3) High and low scores on a value differed considerably in respect of retention of words related to the same value. (4) Different value-oriented subjects did differ with regard to their retention of differently valued words. (5) The joint effect of value orientation and induced frustration did not yield significant effect, but the effect of the frustration treatment on retention with respect to type and degree of value orientation was found significant.

17. Frustration and Achievement Motivation

Gyanoni, T. C. (1984) noticed that most of the subjects of the parent population were not very aggressive or passive in frustrating situations. Boys with high achievement motivation were intropunitive and need persistent, but low in extrapunitive and 'O-D' behaviour. The boys with a low level of achievement motivation were found to be more ego-defensive, obstacle dominant and impunitive in their behaviour.

Dubey, P. (1980) found that the level of motivation decreased at a particular stage of frustration.

18. Frustration and Creativity

Singh, R. P. (1979) reported that:

- Creativity was found to be positively and significantly related to total, social and educational adjustments, but creativity was not found to be significantly related to emotional adjustment;
- No significant relationship was found between creativity and frustration-reactions, i.e., regression, fixation, resignation and aggression;
- No significant relationship was found between creativity and the level of aspiration;
- The high and low creative students were found to differ significantly in their total emotional and educational adjustments. But, they were not found to differ significantly in their social adjustment;
- The high and low creative students were not found to differ significantly in their regression, fixation and resignation, but were found to differ significantly in their aggression;
- The high and low creative students were not found to differ significantly in their level of aspiration;
- All the predicators, viz., adjustment, frustration-reactions and the level of aspiration were not found to influence creativity in the same manner. The role of adjustment, aggression and the level of aspiration was positive nature but dissimilar in numerical weights. The role of regression, fixation and resignation was found to be negative in nature but dissimilar in numerical weights;
- The value of multiple regressions co-efficient between creativity and adjustment, aggression and aspiration was found to be significant, while the other co-efficient were not found to be significant.

19. Frustration and Scheduled Caste Adolescents

Dubey, S. N. (1982) found that:

- The Scheduled Caste (SC) young adults did not differ significantly on any category of reaction to frustrations from the control group of non-SC young adults;
- The SC adolescents had significantly higher mean on ego-defensive and extra aggressive reactions but lower on need persistive, introgressive and irregressive reactions as compared to the non-SC ones. There was an identical reaction pattern among the two caste groups;.
- The SC adolescents and young adults were, by and large, similar in the way they reacted in a frustrating situation except that the young adults had significantly higher mean on obstacle dominance (OD) and lower on need persistence as compared to the adolescents. There was a high degree of parallelism in the reaction pattern of the two castes;
- The non-SC young adults differed significantly from adolescents on five reactions. They had significantly higher mean on obstacle dominance, ego defence and introgressive reactions;
- The OD reactions of the SC adolescents had significant correlation with personality characteristics like happy-go-lucky (factor F+) only. The OD responses of SC young adults were significantly and negatively correlated with personality factors A, F, G, M, Q1 ,Q2, Q4 and positively with I;
- Reservedness, sobriety, expediency, carefulness, conservation, group dependence, tense and tender-mindedness were found to be the personality characteristics of the OD responses;
- OD responses of non-SC adolescents were characterised by reservedness (factor A), threat-sensitivity (factor H) and low integration (factor Q3);

- Non-SCs giving on responses were found to have need for independence and friendliness while SCs had need for independence and low persistence;
- Personality factors A, D and H were negatively correlated with ego defense (ED) responses of SC adolescents;
- ED responses were negatively correlated with factors A, I and positively with N. Reservedness, self-reliance and shrewdness were the personality characteristics of ED responses. Among SC students personality factor A, was found to be consistently and negatively correlated with ED responses in both the age groups;
- Personality factors A,C and I was negatively and E, L, O and Q4 positively related with ED reactions of non-SC young adults.

20. Frustration and Scheduled Castes and Scheduled Tribes

Manharlal, Rajyaguru Balakrishna (1992) reported that:

- The boys were found to be more confirmative with their groups as compared to girls. The SC/ST students with parental education above SSC were found to be more confirmative with their groups in comparison to their counterparts;
- The average scores of SE Pattern-1 of the students with illiterate parents and students with one or two siblings were higher than those of their counterparts.
- The average scores of SE Pattern-2 of:

  (i) Students with high intelligence

  (ii) Boys

  (iii) Students above 21 years of age

  (iv) Students who had graduated

  (v) Students having second or third birth order

  (vi) College students

  (vii) SC/ST students of the science stream were higher than those of their counterparts.

This means that the students of these groups had a higher tendency to blame others.

- The average score of SE Pattern 3 of:
  - (i) Students with low intelligence
  - (ii) Students at average intelligence
  - (iii) SC/ST boys
  - (iv) Girls
  - (v) Students having three or four of siblings
  - (vi) The SC/ST students having the fourth or above birth order
  - (vii) Students of 25-28 years age
  - (viii) SC/ST students of the middle income group
  - (ix) Students of higher secondary
  - (x) SC/ST art students were higher than those of their counterparts

This means that the students of these groups had a higher tendency for self-criticism and blamed their own selves.

- The average scores of SE Pattern-4 of:
  - (i) The other boys
  - (ii) The SC/ST girls
  - (iii) Other students whose fathers were illiterate
  - (iv) SC/ST students having one or two siblings
  - (v) The students having one or the fourth or above birth order
  - (vi) Low income group
  - (vii) Higher secondary students
  - (viii) Arts stream students
  - (ix) Commerce stream students, were higher than those of their counterparts

This means that they had defensive tendency by either excluding some one else or by excluding oneself.

- The trends of directions of aggression and reaction types indicated that more than 47 per cent of the students had trend 'none' at different levels of social status and then moderator variables. This means that the majority of the students did not change their directions of aggression and reaction during attempting all items of the test;
- A larger number of SC/ST students— those with low IQ, girls, those in the age-level 18-21 years, those were illiterate fathers, and those with one or more siblings— had a negative trend of extrapunitive (E) direction of aggression. This means that the extrapunitiveness of these groups of SC/ST students was predominate in the second half (21-40). While the (E) direction of aggression of these groups of other students was predominant in the port (1-20). Moreover, in the SC/ST students of these groups, extrapunitiveness increased as they faced more frustrating situations. The ex of other students of these groups decreased as they faced more frustrations.
- A large number of SC/ST students—those with social status, girls, those above 18 years of age, those with low achievement level, those with father's education at SSC level, those at college level, those in the commerce stream, and those in the science stream—showed appositive trend of ego-defense (ED) while a larger number of others students in these groups had the negative trend of ED type of reaction.

This means that the reaction type ED of these groups, i.e., SC/ST students, is predominant in the first half (1-20), while the reaction type ED of the students of these groups was predominant in other half (21-40). In the SC/ST students of these groups, the reaction type ED increased as they faced more frustrating situations. The reaction type ED of the other students of these groups decreased as they faced more frustrating situations.

21. Frustration and Personality Development

Dubey, P. (1980) reported that:

- Defence mechanisms were applied by these individuals to adjust themselves to the situation. Over confidence developed in the successful subjects' projection, withdrawal, regression, displacement and compensation were the observed defense mechanisms;

- The frustrated individuals formed aggressive and other reactions against the game; the observer, the judgment and the winners. A negative attitude was formed among the frustrated individuals;
- Intelligent subjects, who were frustrated, showed a high degree of conflict, more displacement and a low degree of motivation as compared to normal frustrated group. There was a greater effect of frustration among the intelligent group;
- The frustrated individuals were more affected by suggestions. Suggestions helped them in decreasing the degree of conflict;
- Frustration becomes the cause for another motivation for the next drive to achieve success;
- During frustration, the subjects looked for suggestions that could positively affect them. Unsuccessful students did not accept suggestions;
- The frustrated individuals took more time than the successful group to select an alternative for their drive to draw wooden squares. A high degree of conflict existed.

22. Frustration and Frustrated and Non-frustrated Students

Mithal, S. L. (1975) reported that:

- The frustrated college students expressed their aggression mainly towards the external environment or towards the self while the non-frustrated crossed over situations and were not so hypersensitive as to find it necessary to ventilate their aggression in outward channels or hold themselves responsible for the frustrating situations;
- The two groups differed significantly in different directions; the frustrated students have more frequent

and intense (frequent) extragressive and introgressive reactions than the non-frustrated and the non-frustration have more intense and frequent unaggressive reactions;

- The relationship between frustration and aggression indicated an inverse relationship between group conformity rating GCR scores and aggression manifested in external direction while there was a moderate inverse relationship between GCR scores and aggression manifested towards self; there existed direct relationship between GCR scores and ingression which implied that frustration was related to direction and intensity of aggression. The higher the extent of frustration the greater the extent of aggression either in extra-aggressive direction or in intro-aggressive direction, there was no difference between the degree and post-graduate students with regard to relationship of extent of frustration amount and direction of aggression;
- The frustrated boys were predominantly extra-aggressive while the girls were ingressive, the difference between the boys and the girls' behaviour was significant, this was true of boys and girls of graduate level also;
- P.G. students' frequent reactions and intense reactions were extra-aggressive while those of the degree students were inagressive;
- Student's reactions to religious and social situations were extra-aggressive while those to college and recreational situations were less extra-aggressive; the maximum amount of intro-aggressive reactions were to college situations, the others, in defending order were social, family, recreational and religious ones. The maximum inagressive reactions were in family situations, followed by recreational, college, religious and social situations;
- Extra-aggression was least in family situation when compared to the other situations extra-aggression was maximum in religious situations when compared to

college, recreations and social situations while when extra-aggressive scores were compared in college situations to recreational and social situations, there was no difference between the first two;

- Comparison of intro-aggressive reactions between family, religious and college situations, they were least in religious and highest in college situations while comparison of reactions to family situation with recreations and social situation, the difference was negligible, the intro-aggression was least in recreational and highest in college situation and when reactions to recreation and facilities were compared to social situation, there were little difference in intro-aggressions;
- Students in family situation were most inagressive rather than in the other four situations; they did not differ in inagressive reactions to religious and college or religious and social situations; the students had more adaptive reactions towards recreational situations than religious, college and social situation.

23. Frustration and Cognitive and Non-cognitive Variables

Jethwani, P. M. reported that:

- The non-backward class pupils were found to be more frustrated than the backward class pupils;
- The pupils from small families were significantly more frustrated than the pupils from large families;
- The pupils with high intelligence and those with low intelligence had no significant difference between their mean scores. Intelligence was not a factor that caused frustration;
- The pupils having high anxiety were significantly more frustrated than the pupils having less anxiety;
- The pupils of grade X and XI and grade XII differed significantly in their frustrated scores. The pupils of grade XII had the higher frustration scores than the X grade pupils;
- The pupils having high non-achievement were significantly more frustrated than the pupils having low non-achievement;

- The significant interactions were:
  - (a) Grade vs. family size
  - (b) Non-achievement vs. intelligence
  - (c) Non-achievement vs. family size
  - (d) Anxiety vs. family size
  - (e) Anxiety vs. caste
  - (f) Family size vs. caste

24. Frustration and Intelligence

Lidhoo, M. C. and Sapru, A. K. (1989) reported that: (1) Between the high group conformity rating (GCR) and low GCR subjects, there were no significant differences on intelligence; (2) There were significant differences between higher low GCR groups in the area of direction of aggression; (3) Differences were significant as far as super-ego patterns were concerned based on directions of aggression and types of reaction.

Gupta, Deoyani (1990) reported a significant negative correlation between frustration and intelligence.

Jethwani, P. M. found that intelligence was not a factor that caused frustration.

25. Frustration and Working Women

Sharma, U. (1985) reported that:

- Women of all the groups were well adjusted with bank employees showing the best adjustment;
- Teachers showed obstacle-dominance and ego-defence types of aggression directed outwardly towards the environment in frustrating situations to a greater extent than the normative population. In this, they were like office workers and bank employees but unlike nurses and doctors. The whole sample of women, to an extent greater than the normative population, did not accept blame and tried to avoid frustrating situations. They would blame something in the environment exemplifying the ego-defence type of aggression;

- There was no difference in reaction to frustrating situations based on marital status;
- Working women had high hedonistic values, but in other values they were like others in the population. Teachers were unlike nurses, doctors, and bank employees, but like office workers, average in all ten values, amongst the five groups, teachers had the highest religious and aesthetic values and the lowest democratic, economic and hedonistic values;
- There was a significant correlation between frustration, aggression scores and different values;
- Working women with high socio-economic status were optimistic of getting over a frustrating obstacle, whereas those with low socio-economic status tried to avoid it or deny its presence and to blame others;
- Since women teachers' ego dominates their responses, organisations climate in institutions should take cognizance of this and treat them in a sympathetic way;
- Since they are high in religious and aesthetic values women teachers would be more effective for moral education, education in arts/crafts and fine arts.

26. Frustration and Aspiration

Muthayya, B. C. (1960) stated that: (1) Significant but poor correlation were obtained between frustration - reaction categories and measures of aspiration independently; (2) Aspiration patterns had significant association with the frustration-reaction categories (E, I and M), respectively.

With the study theoretical perspectives and studies on frustration, there arises a need to conduct a study to find out the frustration of prospective teachers. Hence, this study.

3

Methodology of Research

"Research design is the arrangement of conditions for collection and analysis of data in a manner that aims to combine relevance to the research purpose with economy in procedure."

—Claires Cltiz

Method of Research

Research is a systematic enquiry seeking facts through objective verifiable methods in order to discover the relationship among them and to deduce from them the broad principles or laws. Therefore, the very success of a research work depends upon collecting the necessary information. Several methods of collecting information are developed to assist the research. Every survey expert has his own ideas of selecting the best method of collecting information. But, it can not be uniform to all. Selection of the method depends on the type of information to be consulted. For the present study, normative survey method is chosen.

Survey means viewing and interpreting things rigorously and comprehensively. Now-a-days, survey method is a popular way of collecting data and analysing the results statistically and systematically. This method is suitable to this study as this one is a status study.

OPERATIONAL DEFINITIONS OF KEY TERMS

The operational definitions of the important key terms used in the present study on "A Study of Frustration of Prospective Teachers" are discussed and defined herewith.

1. Study

Study refers to a systematic investigation which is objective and research-oriented.

2. Prospective Teachers

Student teachers who are studying in Colleges of Education for getting B.Ed. degree from a University are called prospective teachers.

3. Frustration

Frustration is an emotion that occurs in situations where one is blocked from reaching a personal goal. The more important the goal is, the greater is the frustration.

4. Gender

Gender refers to male and female prospective teachers.

5. Locality

Locality refers to rural and urban areas.

6. Methodology

Methodology refers to the method of study under which the student has been admitted into the course. For the present study, arts and science teaching methodologies were considered.

Arts methodology, the student studies Social Studies as the elective subject.

Science methodology, the student studies Biological Science or Physical Science as the elective subject.

7. Educational Qualification

Educational qualification refers to whether the student is a graduate or a post-graduate. For the present study, arts graduates and post-graduates and science graduates and post-graduates were considered.

Graduates: Those who have completed their three years degree course of study in arts or science or commerce as a specialised subject.

Post-Graduates: Those who have completed their two years PG course of study in arts or science or commerce as a specialised subject.

VARIABLES OF THE STUDY

Variables are the conditions or characteristics that the experimenter manipulates, controls or observes. There are mainly three types of variables, namely, independent, dependent and intervening. The independent variables are those variables which do not change on manipulation by the experimenter. The dependent variables are those variables which change on manipulation done by the experimenter. The intervening variables are those variables which are dependent both on dependent and independent variables.

For the present study, the following independent variables are chosen:

1. *Gender:* Male and female prospective teachers;
2. *Locality:* Rural and urban prospective teachers;
3. *Methodology:* Arts and science prospective teachers;
4. *Educational Qualification:* Graduate and post-graduate prospective teachers.

It was found in the previous studies that there existed and not existed a significant difference in the frustration of males and females. So, to know if any difference exists in this study also, the variables 'gender' was considered.

It was found in the previous studies that there existed and as well as not existed a significant difference in the frustration of rural and urban students. So, to know if any difference exists in this study also, the variables 'locality' was considered.

It was found in the previous studies that there existed a significant difference in the frustration of arts and science students. So, to know if any difference exists in this study also, the variables 'methodology' was considered.

Since no previous studies were conducted on the variables namely methodology and educational qualification, to know if any difference exists, in this study the variables methodology of study and educational qualification were considered.

HYPOTHESES OF THE STUDY

Hypothesis is a tentative generalisation which provides basis to the whole study to be tested by facts. It is a shrewd and intelligent guess, supposition, inference, hunch, provisional statement, a tentative generalisation to the existence of some fact, condition or relationship relative to some phenomena which serves to explain already known facts in a given area of knowledge and which guides the search for new truth on the basis of empirical evidence.

In statistical hypothesis, the sample should be representative of the whole population. This can be ensured in random sampling where the units of population have got equal chances of being represented. The hypothesis to be tested in this study is 'null hypothesis'. Ordinarily, a null hypothesis is a statement to believe that there is no relation between or among variables. Once it is formulated, depending on the outcome, it will be either accepted or rejected. For the present study the following hypotheses were framed:

1. There is no frustration in prospective teachers;
2. There is no significant difference in the frustration of male and female prospective teachers;
3. There is no significant difference in the frustration of rural and urban prospective teachers;
4. There is no significant difference in the frustration of arts and science methodology prospective teachers;
5. There is no significant difference in the frustration of graduate and post-graduate prospective teachers.

SAMPLE OF THE STUDY

A sample is a smaller representation of the larger whole. A sample contains primarily sampling units and a slice of the population representing the universe. A sample must possess the following essential characteristics to provide accurate results. They are representativeness, adequacy, homogeneity, lack of bias, smallness in size, accuracy and completeness.

As a sample is a slice of the population, the population for the study refers to all the prospective teachers who undergo one year study during their B.Ed. course in the Colleges of Education of Guntur district.

Sampling is the easiest method of social investigation. The purpose of sampling is to draw inference concerning the universe. There are three elements in the process of sampling. They are selection of the sample, collection of information a drawing inferences. According to Cornell: "Sampling is the process by which a relatively small number of individuals are selected or analysed in order to find out something about the entire population or the universe from which it is selected". In any research, various methods are utilised for selection of samples. After a detailed study of all the methods, the stratified random sampling method was selected for the present study.

Stratified random sampling is applied as this method of selection assures each individual unit in the universe as equal chance of being chosen. This is suitable for the present study as the universe considered for the study is homogenous.

In order to reduce the sampling error, the sample size of 300 was chosen. In this study, the strata divided are represented in the following table: *(See on next page)*.

TOOL OF THE STUDY

A research tool is a tool which has reliability and validity. It is used for the purpose of data collection. Reliability is the degree of consistency that the instrument or procedure demonstrates. Validity is that quality of a data gathering instrument or procedure which enables it to measure what it is supposed to measure.

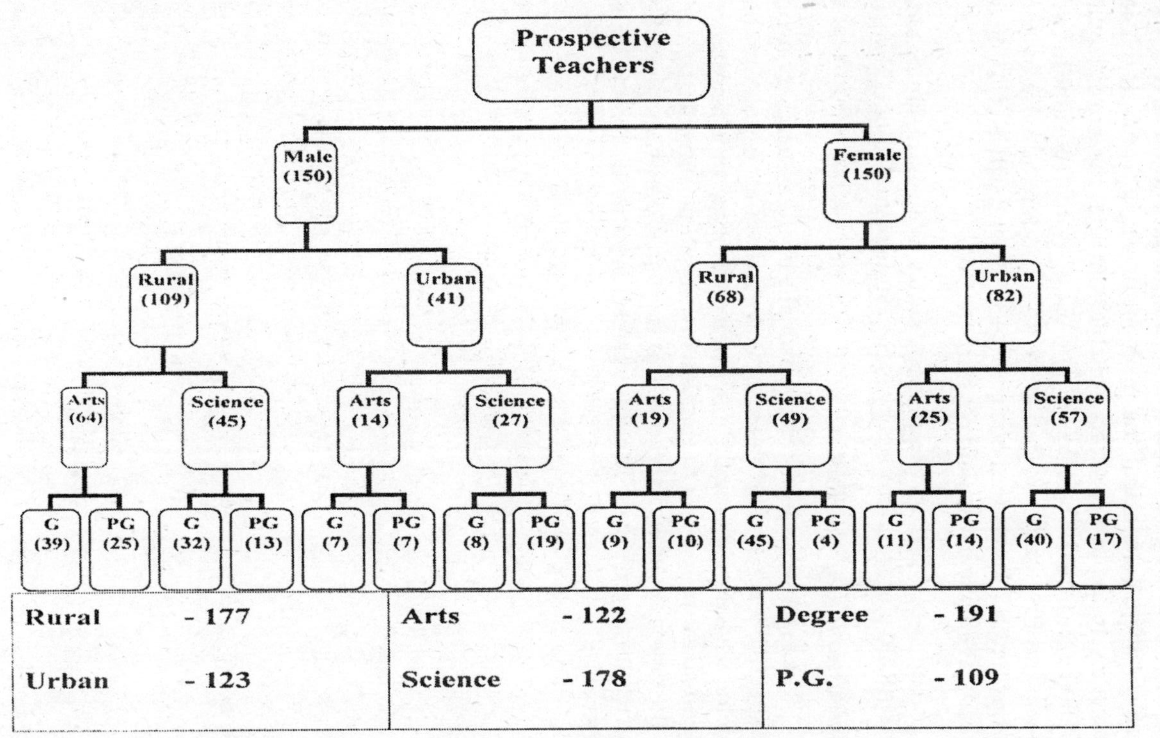
Prospective Teachers
Male (150)
Female (150)
Rural (109)
Urban (41)
Rural (68)
Urban (82)
Arts (64)
Science (45)
Arts (14)
Science (27)
Arts (19)
Science (49)
Arts (25)
Science (57)
G (39)
PG (25)
G (32)
PG (13)
G (7)
PG (7)
G (8)
PG (19)
G (9)
PG (10)
G (45)
PG (4)
G (11)
PG (14)
G (40)
PG (17)
Rural - 177
Urban - 123
Arts - 122
Science - 178
Degree - 191
P.G. - 109

A research tool plays a major role in any worthwhile research, as it is the sole factor in determining sound data and in arriving at perfect conclusions about the problem or study in hand, which ultimately helps in providing suitable remedial measures to the problem concerned. The selection and use of tool can be done in two ways. The first one is to construct a tool independently by the researcher and the second one is to select a standardise tool that is already available in the field of study.

The tool used in the present study is Frustration Scale, constructed and standardised by N.S. Chauhan and Govind Tiwari.

Administration of the Tool

The tool was administered personally by the researcher on the prospective teachers and the sample was asked to respond to the statements. Before giving the tool to the participants, the researcher explained the purpose of the present investigation. Directions given on the cover sheet were read out to the participants and specific instructions were given. The student teachers attended to the scale very well.

4

Analysis of Data

"The analysis and interpretation of data involve the objective material in the possession of the research and his subjective reaction and desires to derive from the data the inherent meanings in their relation to the problem."

—Francis Rummel

Analysis of the data is the most skilled task of all stages of research. It depends on the judgment and skill of the researcher. It should be done by the researcher and should not be entrusted to another person. Analysis of data means studying the tabulated material in order to determine inherent facts or meanings. It involves breaking down complex factors into simple ones and putting the parts in new arrangements for the purpose of interpretation.

The first step in the analysis of data is a critical examination of the assembled data. This includes the researcher to think and analyse the data in the next method of analysis, coding. Coding involves assigning symbols to each response, the purpose of which is to translate raw data into symbols. This depends on proper coding of responses. Coding can be done by the respondent or observer or the interviewer. There may be difficulties in coding due to inadequacy of data, inefficiency of the coder and lack of editing or scrutinising of the available data. Editing can be helpful for coding and for improving the quality of data collection.

Tabulation is a means of recording classification in a compact form in such away so as to facilitate comparisons. Data is arranged in rows and columns to facilitate mathematical and statistical operations. It is of great help in the analysis and interpretation of data. While tabulating the data, the purpose of the study has to be kept in mind.

The method of analysis chosen for a particular study depends upon the nature of objectives, hypotheses to be tested, the purpose and use of the study. Statistical methods are the mathematical techniques used to facilitate the interpretation of numerical data secured from groups of individuals or group of observations or a single individual. A basic knowledge about statistics becomes inevitable for research workers, for systematic analysis and accurate and precise interpretation of data.

For the present study titled "A study of frustration of prospective teachers", several statistical techniques were used to perform the analysis. After collecting the data from three hundred prospective teachers through a standardised tool, the analysis was performed keeping in view the objectives framed, hypotheses formulated, type of tool used, etc. For this purpose, mean, S.D., normal probability, critical ratio, etc., were employed. The highest or the lowest frustration score one can get is 200 or 0 respectively.

Frustration of Prospective Teachers

Hypothesis 1: "There is no frustration in prospective teachers"

To test the validity of hypothesis 1, the mean of the frustration scores was calculated.

Table 4.1: Frustration of Prospective Teachers

Sample	Sample Size	Mean	Standard Deviation
Whole	300	103.87	18.052

From the mean value of Table 4.1, it is evident that there was an average level of frustration in prospective teachers.

The hypothesis that "there is no frustration in prospective teachers" can be rejected as the prospective teachers are possessing an average level of frustration.

Frustration and Gender

Hypothesis 2: "There is no significant difference in the frustration of male and female prospective teachers"

To test the validity of hypothesis 2, the following calculations were carried out.

Table 4.2: Comparison of Frustration Among Male and Female Prospective Teachers

Variable	Sample Size	Mean	S.D.	Mean Difference	Standard Error of Means	Critical Ratio
Male	150	105.56	18.54	3.35	2.078	1.612*
Female	150	102.21	17.45			

* **Not significant at 0.05 level.**

From the values of Table 4.2, it is evident that both male and female prospective teachers were with an average level of frustration without any significant difference between them.

The hypothesis that: "there is no significant difference in the frustration of male and female prospective teachers" can be accepted as there is no significant difference in the level of frustration of male and female prospective teachers.

Frustration and Locality

Hypothesis 3: "There is no significant difference in the frustration of rural and urban prospective teachers"

To test the validity of the hypothesis 3, the following calculations.were made.

Table 4.3: Comparison of Frustration Among Rural and Urban Prospective Teachers

Variable	Sample Size	Mean	S.D.	Mean Difference	Standard Error of Means	Critical Ratio
Rural	177	104.45	17.19	1.41	2.139	0.659*
Urban	123	103.0484	18.91			

* **Not significant at 0.05 level.**

From the values of Table 4.3, it is evident that both rural and urban prospective teachers were with an average level of frustration without any significant difference between them.

The hypothesis that: "There is no significant difference in the frustration of rural and urban prospective teachers" can be accepted as there is no significant difference in the level of frustration of rural and urban prospective teachers.

Frustration and Teaching Methodology

Hypothesis 4: "There is no significant difference in the frustration of arts and science methodology prospective teachers".

To test the validity of hypothesis 4, the following calculations were carried out:

Table 4.4: Comparison of Frustration Among Arts and Science Methodology Prospective Teachers

Variable	Sample Size	Mean	S.D.	Mean Difference	Standard Error of Means	Critical Ratio
Arts Teachers	122	106.48	18.31	4.7	2.123	2.213+
Science Teachers	178	101.78	17.73			

\+ **Significant at 0.05 level.**

From the values of Table 4.4, it is evident that the frustration level in arts and science methodology prospective teachers was significantly different, though both of them possessed an average level of frustration. The arts teaching methodology prospecting teachers were more frustrated that the science methodology prospective teachers.

The hypothesis that "there is no significant difference in the frustration of arts and science methodology prospective teachers" can be rejected as there is a significant difference in the level of frustration of arts and science methodology prospective teachers.

Frustration and Educational Qualification

Hypothesis 5: "There is no significant difference in the frustration of graduate and post-graduate prospective teachers"

To test the validity of hypothesis 5, the following calculations were calculated.

Table 4.5: Comparison of frustration among Graduate and Post-Graduate Prospective Teachers

Variable	Sample Size	Mean	S.D.	Mean Difference	Standard Error of Means	Critical Ratio
Graduate	191	105.1878	16.54	3.013	2.29	1.35*
Post-Graduate	109	101.1748	20.41			

* **Not Significant at 0.05 level.**

From the values of Table 4.5, it is evident that graduate and post-graduate prospective teachers were with average frustration. There was no significant difference between them in the level of frustration possessed.

The hypothesis that: "There is no significant difference in the frustration of graduate and post-graduate prospective teachers" can be accepted as there is no significant difference in the level of frustration of graduate and post-graduate prospective teachers.

5

Summary, Conclusions, Discussion and Suggestions

"Research is perhaps the only assurance we have that a discipline or a profession will not decay into meaningless scraps of dogmatic utterance."

—Bruce W. Tuchman

Summary

Human beings try to fulfill their needs in order to live happily and function effectively, but these needs cannot always be adequately satisfied on account of several obstacles and obstructions. These obstructions cause frustration and produce tension.

The word frustration, now in common usage, refers to the state of someone who denies himself, or who is denied, drive satisfaction. Freud used the word "frustrane", a word probably formed from the German verb "frustrieren", which was in every day usage. The German language has no equivalent to the substantive for "frustration", which was later used in English.

Frustration is an emotion that occurs in situations, where one is blocked from reaching a personal goal. The more important is the goal, the greater is the frustration.

In today's competitive scenario, every person has his targets that he wanted to achieve timely and if he is not able to achieve his targets he is frustrated. This frustration can affect the mind in negative way in which person's thinking power gets slowed down. Frustration leads a person take wrong decisions and as a result of which he is not able to come with innovative ideas. He is not able to achieve all his targets and is left with only his uncompleted plans and unachieved targets. Such a frustrated person goes far away from reality.

Warning signs to frustration are shortness of breath, knot in the throat, stomach cramps, chest pains, headache, excessive alcohol consumption, increased smoking, lack of patience, desire to strike out, etc.

Every one who has any goals experiences frustration and disappointment. One must choose handling frustration by following relaxation techniques, communicating assertively, claiming down physically, modifying thoughts, asking for help, make time for yourself, take care of yourself and seek outside support.

Learn to recognise the warning signs of frustration, intervene to calm yourself down physically, modify your thoughts in a way that reduce your stress, learn to communicate assertively, fix goals as per their abilities and necessities and dare to ask for help in order to prevent frustration.

Frustration has important implications for personality development. Frustrating conditions are an integral part of our development from birth to death and are inevitable in our daily life. Frustration does not always lead to anger and aggressive behaviour, but also diverts the individual towards goal attainment.

Finally, 'frustration ends when adjustment is secured'. However, frustration is a necessary experience in the half of any child and adult, a necessary accompaniment of the processes of growing up. It can stimulate greater efforts at productivity and creativity. If it is not in excess if we have developed the ability to tolerate frustration. This ability is called frustration-tolerance.

The present study is intended to find out the level of frustration of prospective teachers. The sample was drawn from the prospective teachers studying in Colleges of Education situated in Guntur district. The sample size chosen for the present study was 300 (three hundred) prospective teachers.

The objectives of the study were: (1) To find out the frustration of prospective teachers; (2) To compare the frustration of male and female prospective teachers; (3) To compare the frustration of rural and urban prospective teachers; (4) To compare the frustration of arts and science teaching methodology prospective teachers; and (5) To compare the frustration of graduate and post-graduate prospective teachers.

The normative survey method was used for this study. This method investigates into the conditions and relationships that exist at present in the context of frustration.

For the present study, the variables chosen were: (1) Gender (Male and Female Prospective Teachers); (2) Locality (Rural and Urban Prospective Teachers); (3) Teaching methodology (Arts and Science Teaching Methodology Prospective Teachers); and (4) Educational qualification (Graduate and Post-graduate Prospective Teachers).

Hypotheses formulated for the present study were: (1) There is no frustration in prospective teachers; (2) There is no significant difference in the frustration of male and female prospective teachers; (3) There is no significant difference in the frustration of rural and urban prospective teachers; (4) There is no significant difference in the frustration of arts and science methodology prospective teachers; (5) There is no significant difference in the frustration of graduate and post-graduate prospective teachers.

A sample is a small group which represents all the traits and characteristics of the population. The prospective teachers studying in Colleges of Education of Guntur district were selected as population. The stratified random sampling technique was used in selecting the sample. The size of the sample was 300 (three hundred) prospective teachers.

A research tool is a tool used for the purpose of data collection. The tool used in the present study was Frustration Scale, constructed and standardised by N.S. Chauhan, and Govind Tiwari.

For the analysis of data, suitable statistical techniques like mean, S.D., and critical ratio were used.

CONCLUSIONS AND DISCUSSION

From the analysis of the data, the following conclusions are drawn and these are followed by necessary discussion:

1. The prospective teachers were holding an average level of frustration.

The present status of frustration may be due to the nature of course work as the prospective teachers encounter totally a new content as well as new practical experience in teaching, which was not experienced till now. This may also be due to the awareness that the mastery of the subject matter of pedagogy helps in getting a teacher job through the selection test conducted by the government, for which the prospective teachers need to learn and work more when compared to their previous education.

The prospective teachers may overcome this frustration by developing better study habits, by participating in all pedagogical activities intensively, by participating in yoga, meditation etc., by developing achievement motivation and by enhancing academic performance. The frustration can also be overcome by following relaxation techniques and mingling with co-students in performing different kinds of academic activities as per norms and standards laid down in the course work.

2. The male and female prospective teachers had an average level of frustration without any significant difference between them.

Because of the same mental maturity, personality, surrounding environment, aspirations and attitudes, etc., might have played their legitimate role in having a no significant difference in the level of frustration by male and female prospective teachers.

Both male and female prospective teachers should identify their position in teaching and learning area in order to reduce their frustration levels, and develop life skills, coping strategies and proper adjustment in order to reduce their frustration levels.

3. The rural and urban prospective teachers hold an average level of frustration without any significant difference between them.

As the prospective teachers of rural and urban localities strive equally for better achievement in pedagogical activities, they should reduce the level of frustration by following frustration reduction strategies in order to master the subject matter.

4. The prospective teachers of arts and science teaching methodology possessed an average level of frustration with a significant difference between them. The arts teaching methodology prospective teachers were more frustrated than their counterparts.

The science and arts students perceive and have a different kind of knowledge of general education and teacher education. So, both of them differ significantly at their frustration levels. These people should also reduce or avoid the frustration and become good teachers.

5. The graduate and post-graduate prospective teachers were with an average level of frustration with no significant difference between them.

One can expect a difference in the level of frustration in the sub-samples as they differ significantly in knowledge, age and maturation. But, this study does not find any difference in the level of frustration of graduate and post-graduate prospective teachers, due to common course work, which is a good sign in teacher education.

The graduate and post-graduate teachers should minimise the level of frustration that appears in any kind of activity and education so that they can prove as the best teachers.

6. **The prospective teachers studying in colleges of education are with an average level of frustration. Except teaching methodology, the gender, the locality, and the qualification of prospective teachers did not show any influence on the level of frustration of prospective teachers.**

The prospective teachers, the teacher educators and the social and educational environments should make the prospective teachers feel comfortable during their course period. The prospective teachers should identify the reasons for frustration and should attend to those problems by which they can avoid or at least minimize the level of frustration. Better skills, good relations with peer groups and teachers will help the prospective teachers in avoiding of reducing frustration. Relaxation techniques, yoga and meditation, better study habits, good life skills, appropriate aspirations, etc., may also help in reducing the frustration levels of prospective teachers. The prospective teachers should avoid frustration in order to master the knowledge and skills of teacher education and to become expert teachers in future after rolling out of the Colleges of Education.

SUGGESTIONS FOR FURTHER RESEARCH

The present study, "A Study of Frustration of Prospective Teachers," brings to light a good number of new areas to be studied by future researchers. The areas and variables that are not covered by this study may be put to test to enlighten the other associated factors. So, the researchers may think of the following areas of study in detail:

1. This study can be extended to students of all secondary school classes, Intermediate, graduation and post-graduation at district and state levels;
2. Research can be taken up to know the effect of factors like age, stage of education, adjustment, attitude, motivation, creativity and other personality factors on frustration;
3. Studies can be taken up to know the influence of frustration on examination and achievement;

4. Studies can be considered to know the impact of education, employment, economic status, etc., of parents on the frustration of children;

5. Studies can be undertaken to find out the influence of school environment, teachers and co-students on the frustration of students.

Bibliography

Aggarwal, J.C. (2004). *Essentials of Educational Psychology*. New Delhi: Vikas Publishing House Private Limited.

Best, Jhon W. and James V. Khan (2005). *Research in Education*, 9th Edition. New Delhi: Prentice-Hall of India Private Limited.

Bhatia, K.K. (2003). *Bases of Educational Psychology*. New Delhi: Kalyani Publishers.

Bhatia, K.K., and P. Yakaiah (2003). *Introduction to Educational Psychology*. New Delhi: Kalyani Publishers.

Buch, M.B., Editor (1978-1983). *Third Survey of Research in Education*. Baroda: CASE, M.S. University of Baroda.

Buch, M.B., Editor (1983-1988). *Fourth Survey of Research in Education*. New Delhi: NCERT.

Buch, M.B., Editor (1988-1992). *Fifth Survey of Research in Education*. New Delhi: NCERT.

Chauhan, S.S. (1995). *Advanced Educational Psychology*. New Delhi: Vikas Publishing House Private Limited.

Dandapani, S. (2001). *Advanced Educational Psychology*. New Delhi: Anmol Publications Private Limited.

Dash, M., Neena Dash (2006). *Fundamentals of Educational Psychology*. New Delhi: Atlantic Publishers.

Diane E. Papalia and Sally Wendkos Olds (1987). *Psychology*. New York: Fong and Sons Printers Private Limited.

Govind, Tiwari (1984). *Abnormal Psychology.* Agra: Vinod Pustak Mandir.

Kumar (2001). *Abnormal Psychology*. Agra: Lakshmi Narain Agarwal, Educational Publishers.

Kuppuswamy, B. (2003). *Advanced Educational Psychology*. New Delhi: Sterling Publishers Private Limited.

Mangal, S.K. (1984). *Abnormal Psychology*. New Delhi: Sterling Publishers Private Limited.

Mangal, S.K. (1998). *Educational Psychology*. Ludhiana: Prakash Brothers.

Norman L. Munn., Dodge Fernald J.R.L., Fernald, Peters H.S. (1967). *Introduction to Psychology*. New Delhi: Oxford and IBH Publishing Co. Private Limited.

Rachana, Sharma (2004). *Abnormal Psychology*. New Delhi: Atlantic Publishers.

Sharma, Ram Nath and Rachana Sharma (2006). *History and Schools of Psychology*. New Delhi: Atlantic Publishers.

Sharma, Ram Nath and R.K. Sharma (2006). *Advanced Educational Psychology*. Atlantic Publishers.

Siddhu, Kulbir Singh (1990). *Methodology of Research in Education*. New Delhi: Sterling Publishers Private Limited.

Silverman, Robert E. (1978). *Psychology*. New Delhi: Prentice-Hall of India Private Limited.

Srivastava, D.M. (1985). *Abnormal Psychology*. Agra: Vinod Pustak Mandir.

Srivastava, D.N. (1985). *General Psychology*. Agra: Vinod Pustak Mandir.

Witting Arno, F. and Gurney Williams III (1984). *Psychology: An Introduction*. New York: Fong and Sons Prenters Private Limited.

Additional References

Bhaskara Rao, Digumarti (1994). *Scientific Aptitude*. New Delhi: Ashish Publishing House. ISBN 81-7024-658-X.

Bhaskara Rao, Digumarti (1995). *Animal Kingdom*. New Delhi: Discovery Publishing House. ISBN 81-7141-274-2.

Bhaskara Rao, Digumarti (1995). *Batracology*. New Delhi: Discovery Publishing House. ISBN 81-7141-279-3.

Bhaskara Rao, Digumarti (1997). *Scientific Attitude*. New Delhi: Discovery Publishing House. ISBN 81-7141-381-1.

Bhaskara Rao, Digumarti (1996). *Scientific Attitude vis-à-vis Scientific Aptitude*. New Delhi: Discovery Publishing House. ISBN 81-7141-308-0.

Bhaskara Rao, Digumarti (2004). *Scientific Attitude, Scientific Aptitude and Achievement*. New Delhi: Discovery Publishing House. ISBN 81-7141-781-7.

Bhaskara Rao, Digumarti (2004). *Educational Administration*. New Delhi: Discovery Publishing House. ISBN 81-7141-842-2.

Bhaskara Rao, Digumarti (2004). *Issues in School Education*. New Delhi: Discovery Publishing House. ISBN 81-8356-025-3.

Bhaskara Rao, Digumarti, Editor (1996). *Encyclopaedia of Education For All*, 5 Volumes. New Delhi: APH Publishing Corporation. ISBN 81-7024-759-4 (set).

Vol. I *Education For All: The World Conference*. ISBN 81-7024-760-8

Vol. II *Education For All: The EPA-9 Summi*t. ISBN 81-7024-761-6

Vol. III *Education For All: Quality Education For All*. ISBN 81-7024-762-6.

Vol. IV *Education For All: Planning and Monitoring*. ISBN 81-7024-763-4.

Vol. V *Education For All: The Indian Scenario*. ISBN 81-7024-764-0.

Bhaskara Rao, Digumarti, Editor (1996). *National Policy on Education*, 2 Volumes. New Delhi: Anmol Publications Pvt. Ltd. ISBN 81-7488-323-1.

Bhaskara Rao, Digumarti, Editor (1996). *Global Perceptions on Peace Education*, 3 Volumes. New Delhi: Discovery Publishing House. ISBN 81-7141-319-6.

Bhaskara Rao, Digumarti, Editor (1997). *Education for the 21st Century*. New Delhi: Discovery Publishing House. ISBN 81-7141-389-7.

Bhaskara Rao, Digumarti, Editor (1997). *Reflections on Scientific Attitude*. New Delhi: Discovery Publishing House. ISBN 81-7141-319-6.

Bhaskara Rao, Digumarti, Editor (1997). *Success Story of a Primary Education Project*. New Delhi: APH Publishing Corporation. ISBN 81-7024-850-7.

Bhaskara Rao, Digumarti, Editor (1997). *World Food Summit*. New Delhi: Discovery Publishing House. ISBN 81-7141-386-2.

Bhaskara Rao, Digumarti, Editor (1997). *Care the Child*, 2 Volumes. New Delhi: Discovery Publishing House. ISBN 81-7141-394-3.

Bhaskara Rao, Digumarti, Editor (1998). *Earth Summit*, 2 Volumes. New Delhi: Discovery Publishing House. ISBN 81-7141-435-4.

Bhaskara Rao, Digumarti, Editor (1998). *Adolescence Education*. New Delhi: Discovery Publishing House. ISBN 81-7141-432-X.

Bhaskara Rao, Digumarti, Editor (1998). *Community and School Nutrition Education*. New Delhi: Discovery Publishing House. ISBN 81-7141-435-4.

Bhaskara Rao, Digumarti, Editor (1998). *District Primary Education Programme*. New Delhi: Discovery Publishing House. ISBN 81-7141-396-X.

Bhaskara Rao, Digumarti, Editor (1998). *National Policy on Education: Towards an Enlightened and Humane Society*. New Delhi: Discovery Publishing House. ISBN 81-7141-426-5.

Bhaskara Rao, Digumarti, Editor (1998). *Reforming School Education*. New Delhi: Discovery Publishing House. ISBN 81-7141-403-6.

Bhaskara Rao, Digumarti, Editor (1998). *Teacher Education in India*. New Delhi: Discovery Publishing House. ISBN 81-7141-406-0.

Bhaskara Rao, Digumarti, Editor (1998). *World Summit for Social Development*. New Delhi: Discovery Publishing House. ISBN 81-7141-420-6.

Bhaskara Rao, Digumarti, Editor (1999). *International Encyclopaedia of AIDS*, 11 Volumes. New Delhi: Discovery Publishing House. ISBN 81-7141-522-6 (set).

Vol. 1 *Introduction to HIV/AIDS*. ISBN 81-7141-523-7.

Vol. 2 *HIV/AIDS—Issues and Challenges*, 2 Parts. ISBN 81-7141-524-5.

Vol. 3 *HIV/AIDS—Socio Economic Realities*. ISBN 81-7141-524-3.

Vol. 4 *HIV/AIDS—Law Ethics and Human Rights*, 2 Parts. ISBN 81-7141-526-1.

Vol. 5 *AIDS and NGOs*. ISBN 81-7141-527-X.

Vol. 6 *AIDS and Home Care*. ISBN 81-7141-528-8.

Vol. 7 *STD Case Management*. ISBN 81-7141-529-6.

Vol. 8 *HIV/AIDS Prevention and Care—Teaching Modules for Nurses and Midwives*. ISBN 81-7141-530-X.

Vol. 9 *HIV Prevention Education for Educational Institutions*. ISBN 81-7141-531-8.

Vol. 10 *Instructional Modules for AIDS Education*. ISBN 81-7141-532-6.

Vol.11 *School Health Education to Prevent AIDS and STD—A Package for Curriculum Planners*. ISBN 81-7141-533-4.

Bhaskara Rao, Digumarti, Editor (2000). *International Encyclopaedia of Human Rights*, 7 Volumes in 13 Parts. New Delhi: Discovery Publishing House. ISBN 81-7141-567-9 (set).

Vol. 1 *International Instruments of Human Rights*, 2 Parts. ISBN 81-7141-569-4.

Vol. 2 *Regional Instruments of Human Rights*. ISBN 81-7141-604-7.

Vol. 3 *Human Rights and the United Nations,* 2 Parts. ISBN 81-7141-605-5.

Vol. 4 *Fact Files of Human Rights,* 3 Parts. ISBN 81-7141-606-3.

Vol. 5 *Study Stories of Human Rights,* 3 Parts. ISBN 81-7141-607-3.

Vol. 6 *International Meetings on Human Rights,* 2 parts. ISBN 81-714-608-X.

Vol. 7 *Professional Training in Human Rights.* ISBN 81-7141-609-8.

Bhaskara Rao, Digumarti, Editor (2000). *International Encyclopaedia of Science and Technology Education,* 11 Volumes. New Delhi: Discovery Publishing House. ISBN 81-7141-548-2 (set).

Vol. 1 *Science and Technology Education.* ISBN 81-7141-568-7.

Vol. 2 *Science Education in Developing Countries.* ISBN 81-7141-569-9.

Vol. 3 *Organisational Structure of Science.* ISBN 81-7141-570-9.

Vol. 4 *Science Education in Asia and the Pacific.* ISBN 81-7141-571-7.

Vol. 5 *Science and Technology Education For All.* ISBN 81-7141-572-5.

Vol. 6 *Values, Ethics, Talent and Girls in Science and Technology Education.* ISBN 81-7141-573-3.

Vol. 7 *Popularization of Science and Technology Education.* ISBN 81-7141-574-1.

Vol. 8 *Science, Power and Society.* ISBN 81-7141- 575-X.

Vol. 9 *Information Technology.* ISBN 81-7141-576-8.

Vol. 10 *Teacher Training in Science and Technology Education.* ISBN 81-7142-577-6.

Vol. 11 *Teacher Training in Science and Technology: A Curriculum Framework.* ISBN 81-7141-578-4.

Bhaskara Rao, Digumarti, Editor (2000). *Education For All: Achieving the Goal,* 3 Volumes. New Delhi: APH Publishing Corporation. ISBN 81-7648-152-1 (set).

Vol. I *The Global Consensus*. ISBN 81-7648-155-6.

Vol. II *Mid-Decade Review Reports of Regional Seminars*. ISBN 81-7648- 154-8.

Vol. III *Issues and Trends*. ISBN 81-7648-155-6.

Bhaskara Rao, Digumarti, Editor (2001). *Nuclear Materials: Issues and Concerns*, 2 Volumes. New Delhi: Discovery Publishing House. ISBN 81-7141-611-X.

Bhaskara Rao, Digumarti, Editor (2001). *Distance Education in Different Countries*. New Delhi: APH Publishing Corporation. ISBN 81-7648-229-3.

Bhaskara Rao, Digumarti, Editor (2001). *Decentralised Management of Education: Management of Education in Panchayati Raj and Municipal Bodies*. New Delhi: Discovery Publishing House. ISBN 81-7141-617-9.

Bhaskara Rao, Digumarti, Editor (2001). *Electrochemistry for Environmental Protection*. New Delhi: Discovery Publishing House. ISBN 81-7141-619-5.

Bhaskara Rao, Digumarti, Editor (2001). *Global Educational Studies*. New Delhi: Discovery Publishing House. ISBN 81-7141-616-0.

Bhaskara Rao, Digumarti, Editor (2001). *Global Synthesis of Educational Assessment*. New Delhi: Discovery Publishing House. ISBN 81-7141-613-6.

Bhaskara Rao, Digumarti, Editor (2001). *Jomtein Decade of Education*. New Delhi: Discovery Publishing House. ISBN 81-7141-618-7.

Bhaskara Rao, Digumarti, Editor (2001). *World Conference on Education for All*. New Delhi: Discovery Publishing House. ISBN 81-7141-274-9.

Bhaskara Rao, Digumarti, Editor (2001). *World Conference on Higher Education*. New Delhi: Discovery Publishing House. ISBN 81-7141-610-1.

Bhaskara Rao, Digumarti, Editor (2001). *World Conference on Science*. New Delhi: Discovery Publishing House. ISBN 81-7141-612-8.

Bhaskara Rao, Digumarti, Editor (2003). *Inspiring Experiences in Teacher Education*. New Delhi: Discovery Publishing House. ISBN 81-7141-656-X.

Bhaskara Rao, Digumarti, Editor (2003). *International Studies in Education*, 3 Volumes. New Delhi: Discovery Publishing House. ISBN 81-7141-647-0.

Bhaskara Rao, Digumarti, Editor (2003). *Military Conversion: Impact on Science and Technology*. New Delhi: Discovery Publishing House. ISBN 81-7141-578-4.

Bhaskara Rao, Digumarti, Editor (2003). *United Nations Millennium Summit*. New Delhi: Discovery Publishing House. ISBN 81-7141-632-2.

Bhaskara Rao, Digumarti, Editor (2003). *World Assembly on Aging*. New Delhi: Discovery Publishing House. ISBN 81-7141-637-3.

Bhaskara Rao, Digumarti, Editor (2003). *World Conference on Human Rights*. New Delhi: Discovery Publishing House. ISBN 81-7141-661-6.

Bhaskara Rao, Digumarti, Editor (2003). *World Education Forum*. New Delhi: Discovery Publishing House. ISBN 81-7141-639-X.

Bhaskara Rao, Digumarti, Editor (2003). Education, *Employment and Human Resource Development*. New Delhi: Discovery Publishing House. ISBN 81-7141- 681-0.

Bhaskara Rao, Digumarti, Editor (2003). *Successful Schooling*. New Delhi: Discovery Publishing House. ISBN 81-7141-677-2.

Bhaskara Rao, Digumarti, Editor (2003). *European Education and Teachers*. New Delhi: Discovery Publishing House. ISBN 81-7141-702-7.

Bhaskara Rao, Digumarti, Editor (2003). *Teachers in a Changing World*. New Delhi: Discovery Publishing House. ISBN 81-7141-694-2.

Bhaskara Rao, Digumarti, Editor (2004). *International Guidelines on Open and Distance Teacher Education*. New Delhi: Discovery Publishing House. ISBN 81-7141-777-9.

Bhaskara Rao, Digumarti, Editor (2004). *Adult Learning in the 21st Century*. New Delhi: Discovery Publishing House. ISBN 81-7141-797-3.

Bhaskara Rao, Digumarti, Editor (2004). *Educational Practices: Research and Recommendations*. New Delhi: Discovery Publishing House. ISBN 81-7141-835-X.

Bhaskara Rao, Digumarti, Editor (2004). *General Secondary Education In the 21st Century*. New Delhi: Discovery Publishing House.

Bhaskara Rao, Digumarti, Editor (2004). *International Encyclopaedia of Learning to Live Together*, 4 Volumes. New Delhi: Discovery Publishing House. ISBN 81-7141-848-1.

Vol. 1 *International Conference on Learning to Live Together.*

Vol. 2 *Globalisation and Living Together.*

Vol. 3 *Curriculum for Learning to Live Together.*

Vol. 4 *Science Education for the Contemporary Society.*

Bhaskara Rao, Digumarti, Editor (2004). *Reforming Secondary Education*. New Delhi: Discovery Publishing House. ISBN 81-7141-843-0.

Bhaskara Rao, Digumarti, Editor (2004). *Human Rights Education*. New Delhi: Discovery Publishing House. ISBN 81-7141-882-1.

Bhaskara Rao, Digumarti, Editor (2004). *United Nations Decade for Human Rights Education*. New Delhi: Discovery Publishing House. ISBN 81-7141-887-2.

Bhaskara Rao, Digumarti, Editor (2004). *Technical and Vocational Education and Training in the 21st Century*. New Delhi: Discovery Publishing House. ISBN 81-7141-984-4.

Bhaskara Rao, Digumarti, Editor (2005). *Encyclopaedia of Education For All*, 5 Volumes. New Delhi: Discovery Publishing House.

Bhaskara Rao, Digumarti and B.S.V. Dutt, Editors (2003). *Education: Programmes and Policies*. New Delhi: APH Publishing Corporation. ISBN 81-7648-470-9.

Bhaskara Rao, Digumarti, C.A.P. Swamy and B.S.V. Dutt (1997). *Self-Evaluation in Student Teaching*. New Delhi: Discovery Publishing House. ISBN 81-7141-374-9.

Bhaskara Rao, Digumarti and D. Naresh Kumar (2004). *School Teacher Effectiveness*. New Delhi: Discovery Publishing House. ISBN 81-7141-782-5.

Bhaskara Rao, Digumarti and D. Sridhar (2002). *Job Satisfaction of School Teachers*. New Delhi: Discovery Publishing House. ISBN 81-7141-652-7.

Bhaskara Rao, Digumarti, C. Sridevi and K. Vijaya (1995). *Achievement in Social Studies*. New Delhi: Discovery Publishing House. ISBN 81-7141-281-5.

Bhaskara Rao, Digumarti and Digumarti Pushpa Latha (1994). *Achievement in Biology*. New Delhi: Discovery Publishing House. ISBN 81-7141-264-5.

Bhaskara Rao, Digumarti and Digumarti Pushpa Latha (1995). *Achievement in English*. New Delhi: Discovery Publishing House. ISBN 81-7141-283-1.

Bhaskara Rao, Digumarti and Digumarti Pushpa Latha (1994). *Achievement in Science*. New Delhi: Discovery Publishing House. ISBN 81-7141-280-70.

Bhaskara Rao, Digumarti and Digumarti Pushpa Latha (1995). *Achievement in Mathematics*. New Delhi: Discovery Publishing House. ISBN 81-7141-278-5.

Bhaskara Rao, Digumarti and Digumarti Pushpa Latha (2004). *Education for Women*. New Delhi: Discovery Publishing House. ISBN 81-7141-873-2.

Bhaskara Rao, Digumarti, Digumarti Pushpa Latha and Digumarthi Harshitha, Editors (2001). *Biological Warfare*. New Delhi: Discovery Publishing House. ISBN 81-7141-597-0.

Bhaskara Rao, Digumarti, Digumarti Pushpa Latha and Digumarthi Harshitha, Editors (2001). *Women As Educators*. New Delhi: Discovery Publishing House. ISBN 81-7141-602-0.

Bhaskara Rao, Digumarti and Digumarthi Harshitha (2004). *Adjustment of Adolescents*. New Delhi: APH Publishing House. ISBN 81-7648-836-8.

Bhaskara Rao, Digumarti and Digumarthi Harshitha, Editors (2001). *Education in India*. New Delhi: APH Publishing House. ISBN 81-7648-207-2.

Bhaskara Rao, Digumarti and Digumarti Pushpa Latha, Editors (1998). *International Encyclopaedia of Women*, 5 Volumes. New Delhi: Discovery Publishing House. ISBN 81-7141-410-9 (set).

Vol. 1 *Status of World's Women*. ISBN 81-7141-494-X.

Vol. 2 *Women, Education and Empowerment*. ISBN 81-7141-498-1.

Vol. 3 *Women Challenges and Advancement*. ISBN 81-7141-497-4.

Vol. 4 *Women and Family Health*. ISBN 81-7141-497-4.

Vol. 5 *Women and International Action*. ISBN 81-7141-498-2.

Bhaskara Rao, Digumarti, Digumarti Pushpa Latha and Digumarthi Harshitha, Editors (2001). *Assessing Learning Achievement*. New Delhi: Discovery Publishing House. ISBN 81-7141-601-2.

Bhaskara Rao, Digumarti, Digumarti Pushpa Latha and Digumarthi Harshitha, Editors (2001). *Energy Security*. New Delhi: Discovery Publishing House. ISBN 81-7141-598-9.

Bhaskara Rao, Digumarti, Digumarthi Harshitha and K.R.S. Sambasiva Rao, Editors (1999). *Advanced Biotechnology*. New Delhi: Discovery Publishing House. ISBN 81-7141-516-4.

Bhaskara Rao, Digumarti and K.R.S. Sambasiva Rao, Editors (1996). *Current Trends in Indian Education*. New Delhi: Discovery Publishing House. ISBN 81-7141-311-0.

Bhaskara Rao, Digumarti and D. Naresh Kumar (2004). *School Teacher Effectiveness*. New Delhi: Discovery Publishing House. ISBN 81-7141-782-5.

Bhaskara Rao, Digumarti and E. Sreekanth Babu (2004). *Educational Interests of School Students*. New Delhi: Discovery Publishing House. ISBN 81-7141-837-6.

Bhaskara Rao, Digumarti and K. Vijaya (1995). *A Text Book Evaluation*. Ambala Cantt: The Associated Publishers.

Bhaskara Rao, Digumarti and M.A. Fayaz (2004). *Problems of Primary School Drop-outs*. New Delhi: Discovery Publishing House. ISBN 81-7141- 834-1.

Bhaskara Rao, Digumarti and N.V.M. Mohana Rao (2002). *Problems of Mentally Handicapped Children*. New Delhi: Discovery Publishing House. ISBN 81-7141- 645-4.

Bhaskara Rao, Digumarti and S. Chandra Mohan (2002). *Sports Management*. New Delhi: APH Publishing House. ISBN 81-7648-467-9.

Bhaskara Rao, Digumarti and S.A. Khader (2004). *Problems of Private School Teachers*. New Delhi: Discovery Publishing House. ISBN 81-7141-838-4.

Bhaskara Rao, Digumarti and S.A. Khader (2004). *School Education in India*. New Delhi: Discovery Publishing House. ISBN 81-7141-849-X.

Bhaskara Rao, Digumarti and Sk. Johni Basha (2004). *Teachers' Population Education Awareness*. New Delhi: Discovery Publishing House. ISBN 81-7141-832-5.

Bhaskara Rao, Digumarti, V.V. Rao, V.V. Lakshmi and V.V. Krishna, Editors (1999). *Status and Advancement of Women*. New Delhi: APH Publishing Corporation. ISBN 81-7648-169-6.

Appala Naidu, P.Ch., Author and Digumarti Bhaskara Rao, Editor (2007). *Feedback Methods and Students Performance*. New Delhi: Discovery Publishing House. ISBN 81-8356-284-1.

Amala, P.A. and Anupama, P., Authors and Digumarti Bhaskara Rao, Editor (2004). *History of Education*. New Delhi: Discovery Publishing House. ISBN 81-7141-860-0.

Babu, P.C., Author and Digumarti Bhaskara Rao, Editor (2004). *Flowers of Wisdom*. New Delhi: Discovery Publishing House. ISBN 81-7141-695-0.

Bujji Babu, K., Author and Digumarti Bhaskara Rao, Editor (2007). *Teaching Aptitude of Primary School Teachers*. New Delhi: Sonali Publications. ISBN 81-8411-083-9.

Bhagya Lakshmi, L., Author and Digumarti Bhaskara Rao, Editor (2000). *Reading and Comprehension*. New Delhi: Discovery Publishing House. ISBN 81-7141-543-1.

Bhasha, S.A., author and Digumarti Bhaskara Rao, Editor (2004). *Methods of Teaching Geography*. New Delhi: Discovery Publishing House. ISBN 81-7141-807-4.

Bhuvaneswara Lakshmi, Gadde, Author and Digumarti Bhaskara Rao, Editor(2000). *Attitude Towards Science*. New Delhi: Discovery Publishing House. ISBN 81-7141-541-6.

Bhuvaneswara Lakshmi, G., Author and Digumarti Bhaskara Rao, Editor (2004). *Methods of Teaching Life Science*. New Delhi: Discovery Publishing House. ISBN 81-7141-804-X.

Bhuvaneswara Lakshmi, G. and K. Subba Rao, Authors and Digumarti Bhaskara Rao, Editor (2004). *Methods of Teaching Biology*. New Delhi: Discovery Publishing House. ISBN 81-7141-914-3.

Bramhaiah, T., Author and Digumarti Bhaskara Rao, Editor (2008). *Stress of Prospective Teachers*. New Delhi: Sonali Publications.

Chary, K.V.N.B., Author and Digumarti Bhaskara Rao, Editor (2006). *Techniques of Teaching Physics*. New Delhi: Sonali Publications. ISBN 81-8411-046-4.

Chowdary, S.B.J.R. and Naga Raju, Authors and Digumarti Bhaskara Rao, Editor (2004). *Mastery of Teaching Skills*. New Delhi: Discovery Publishing House.

Dayakara Reddy, V. and Digumarti Bhaskara Rao, Editors (2006). *Value-oriented Education*. New Delhi: Discovery Publishing House.

Devraj, T.A.S., Author and Digumarti Bhaskara Rao, Editor (1997). *Trace Analysis of Uranium and Thorium*. New Delhi: Discovery Publishing House. ISBN 81-7141-375-7.

Durga Rani, K., Author and Digumarti Bhaskara Rao, Editor (2000). *Educational Aspirations and Scientific Attitudes*. New Delhi: Discovery Publishing House. ISBN 81-7141-555-5.

Dutt, B.S.V. and Digumarti Bhaskara Rao (2001). *Empowering Primary Teachers*. New Delhi: Discovery Publishing House. ISBN 81-7141-615-2.

Dutt, B.S.V., Author and Digumarti Bhaskara Rao, Editor (2004). *Comparative Education*. New Delhi: Discovery Publishing House. ISBN 81-7141-912-7.

Ediger, Marlow and Digumarti Bhaskara Rao (1996). *Science Curriculum*. New Delhi: Discovery Publishing House. ISBN 81-7141-321-8.

Ediger, Marlow and Digumarti Bhaskara Rao (2000). *Teaching Mathematics Successfully*. New Delhi: Discovery Publishing House. ISBN 81-7141-552-0.

Ediger, Marlow and Digumarti Bhaskara Rao (2001). *Teaching Science Successfully*. New Delhi: Discovery Publishing House. ISBN 81-7141-600-4.

Ediger, Marlow and Digumarti Bhaskara Rao (2001). *Teaching Social Studies Successfully*. New Delhi: Discovery Publishing House. ISBN 81-7141-596-2.

Ediger, Marlow and Digumarti Bhaskara Rao (2002). *Philosophy and Curriculum*. New Delhi: Discovery Publishing House. ISBN 81-7141-631-4.

Ediger, Marlow and Digumarti Bhaskara Rao (2002). *Improving School Administration*. New Delhi: Discovery Publishing House. ISBN 81-7141-633-0

Ediger, Marlow and Digumarti Bhaskara Rao (2002). *Elementary Curriculum*. New Delhi: Discovery Publishing House. ISBN 81-7141-658-6.

Ediger, Marlow and Digumarti Bhaskara Rao (2003). *Language Arts Curriculum*. New Delhi: Discovery Publishing House. ISBN 81-7141-657-8.

Ediger, Marlow and Digumarti Bhaskara Rao (2003). *Psychology and Curriculum*. New Delhi: Discovery Publishing House. ISBN 81-7141-691-8.

Ediger, Marlow and Digumarti Bhaskara Rao (2003). *Teaching Language Arts Successfully*. New Delhi: Discovery Publishing House. ISBN 81-7141-768-0.

Ediger, Marlow and Digumarti Bhaskara Rao (2003). School *Curriculum and Administration*. New Delhi: Discovery Publishing House. ISBN 81-7141-709-4.

Ediger, Marlow and Digumarti Bhaskara Rao (2003). *Teaching Mathematics in Elementary Schools*. New Delhi: Discovery Publishing House. ISBN 81-7141-687-X.

Ediger, Marlow and Digumarti Bhaskara Rao (2003). *Teaching Science in Elementary Schools*. New Delhi: Discovery Publishing House. ISBN 81-7141-698-5.

Ediger, Marlow and Digumarti Bhaskara Rao (2003). *School Curriculum and Administration*. New Delhi: Discovery Publishing House. ISBN 81-7141-709-4.

Ediger, Marlow and Digumarti Bhaskara Rao (2003). *Elementary Curriculum Improvement*. New Delhi: Discovery Publishing House. ISBN 81-7141-740-X.

Ediger, Marlow and Digumarti Bhaskara Rao (2004). *School Organisation*. New Delhi: Discovery Publishing House. ISBN 81-7141-843-0.

Ediger, Marlow and Digumarti Bhaskara Rao (2004). *Relevancy in Elementary Curriculum*. New Delhi: Discovery Publishing House. ISBN 81-7141-845-9.

Ediger, Marlow and Digumarti Bhaskara Rao (2005). *Quality School Education*. New Delhi: Discovery Publishing House. ISBN 81-8356-022-9.

Ediger, Marlow and Digumarti Bhaskara Rao (2006). *Successful School Education*. New Delhi: Discovery Publishing House. ISBN 81-8356-054-7.

Ediger, Marlow and Digumarti Bhaskara Rao (2006). *Successful School Administration*. New Delhi: Discovery Publishing House. ISBN 81-8356-046-6.

Ediger, Marlow and Digumarti Bhaskara Rao (2006). *Issues in School Curriculum*. New Delhi: Discovery Publishing House. ISBN 81-8356-052-0.

Ediger, Marlow and Digumarti Bhaskara Rao (2006). *Community College: Curriculum and Teaching*. New Delhi: Discovery Publishing House. ISBN 81-8356-053-9.

Ediger, Marlow and Digumarti Bhaskara Rao (2006). *Administration of Schools*. New Delhi: Discovery Publishing House. ISBN 81-8356-2442.

Ediger, Marlow and Digumarti Bhaskara Rao (2006). *Reading Curriculum and Instruction*. New Delhi: Discovery Publishing House. ISBN 81-8356-266-3.

Ediger, Marlow and Digumarti Bhaskara Rao (2006). *Curriculum Organisation*. New Delhi: Discovery Publishing House.

Ediger, Marlow and Digumarti Bhaskara Rao (2006). *Curriculum of School Subjects*. New Delhi: Discovery Publishing House.

Ediger, Marlow, B.S.V. Dutt and Digumarti Bhaskara Rao (2003). *Teaching English Successfully*. New Delhi: Discovery Publishing House. ISBN 81-7141-707-8.

Ediger, Marlow and Digumarti Bhaskara Rao (2007). *School Science Education*. New Delhi: Discovery Publishing House. ISBN 81-8356-352-X.

Ediger, Marlow and Digumarti Bhaskara Rao (2007). *Language Arts Education*. New Delhi: Discovery Publishing House. ISBN 81-8356-333-3.

Elizabeth, M.E.S., Author and Digumarti Bhaskara Rao, Editor (2004). *Methods of Teaching English*. New Delhi: Discovery Publishing House. ISBN 81-7141-809-0.

Elizabeth, M.E.S., Author and Digumarti Bhaskara Rao, Editor (2004). *Acquisition of English Vocabulary*. New Delhi: Discovery Publishing House. ISBN 81-8356-075-X.

Fatima, Sk. Author and Digumarti Bhaskara Rao, Editor (2007). *Reasoning Ability of School Students*. New Delhi: Discovery Publishing House. ISBN 81-8356-330-9.

Fatima, Sk. and Digumarti Bhaskara Rao (2008). *Reasoning Ability of Adolescent Students*. New Delhi: Sonali Publications.

Gopala Krishna, M., Author and Digumarti Bhaskara Rao, Editor (2007). *Techniques of Teaching Physical Education*. New Delhi: Sonali Publications. ISBN 81-8411-044-8.

Gopala Krishna, M., Author and Digumarti Bhaskara Rao, Editor (2007). *Techniques of Teaching Education*. New Delhi: Sonali Publications. ISBN 81-8411-062-6.

Harshitha, Digumarthi, Author and Digumarti Bhaskara Rao, Editor (2004). *Methods of Teaching Information Technology*. New Delhi: Discovery Publishing House. ISBN 81-7141-805-8.

Harshitha, Digumarthi, Author and Digumarti Bhaskara Rao, Editor (2007). *Techniques of Teaching Computer Science*. New Delhi: Sonali Publications. ISBN 81-8411-036-7.

Indira Devi, Author and J. Prasanth Kumar and Digumarti Bhaskara Rao, Editors (2004). *Values in Language Text Books*. New Delhi: Discovery Publishing House. ISBN 81-7141-833-3.

Jalaja Kumari, C., Author and Digumarti Bhaskara Rao, Editor (2004). *Methods of Teaching Educational Technology*. New Delhi: Discovery Publishing House. ISBN 81-7141-810-4.

Jalaja Kumari, C., Author and Digumarti Bhaskara Rao, Editor (2007). *Job Satisfaction of Teachers*. New Delhi: Discovery Publishing House. ISBN 81-8356-329-5.

Janardhan Reddy, B., Author and Digumarti Bhaskara Rao, Editor (2006). *Techniques of Teaching Sociology*. New Delhi: Sonali Publications. ISBN 81-8411-042-1.

Jayalakshmi, M., Author and Digumarti Bhaskara Rao, Editor (2008). *Microteaching and Prospective Teachers*. New Delhi: Sonali Publications.

Jayasree, K., Author and Digumarti Bhaskara Rao, Editor (1999). *Correlates of Socialisation*. New Delhi: Discovery Publishing House. ISBN 81-7141-517-2.

Jayasree, K., Author and Digumarti Bhaskara Rao, Editor (2004). *Methods of Teaching Science*. New Delhi: Discovery Publishing House. ISBN 81-7141-801-5.

John Babu, C., Author and T.J.R. Prasad, G.M. Madhukar and Digumarti Bhaskara Rao, Editors (2004). *Problem Solving in Mathematics*. New Delhi: APH Publishing Corporation. ISBN 81-7648-273-0.

Joseph Raju, B and G.A. Anitha, Authors and Digumarti Bhaskara Rao, Editor (2004). *Population Education*. New Delhi: Sonali Publications. ISBN 81-88836-31-3.

Lalitha, T., Author and K.S. Prabhakaram, D.S.N. Sastry and Digumarti Bhaskara Rao, Editors (2004). *Educational Philosophic Beliefs*. New Delhi: Discovery Publishing House. ISBN 81-7141-765-5.

Krishna, G., Author and Digumarti Bhaskara Rao, Editor (2006). *Techniques of Teaching Physical Education*. New Delhi: Discovery Publishing House. ISBN 81-8411-044-8.

Kumar Raja, G., Author and Digumarti Bhaskara Rao, Editor (2007). *Principles of Primary School*. New Delhi: Sonali Publications. ISBN 81-8411-054-5.

Lakshmi Kumari, V., Author and Digumarti Bhaskara Rao, Editor (2006). *Techniques of Teaching Home Science*. New Delhi: Sonai Publications. ISBN 81-8411-048-0.

Madhava, K., Author and Digumarti Bhaskara Rao, Editor (2008). *Personality of Adolescent Students*. New Delhi: Sonali Publications. ISBN 81-8356-266-3.

Madhu Bala, Jampala, Author and Digumarti Bhaskara Rao, Editor (2004). *Methods of Teaching Exceptional Children*. New Delhi: Discovery Publishing House. ISBN 81-7141-802-3.

Madhu Bala, Jampala, Author and Digumarti Bhaskara Rao, Editor (2007). *Adjustment Problems of Hearing Impaired*. New Delhi: Discovery Publishing House. ISBN 81-7141-831-7.

Marja, Talvi and Digumarti Bhaskara Rao, Editors (1996). *Educational Leadership and Social Changes*. New Delhi: Discovery Publishing House. ISBN 81-7141-320-X.

Mohana Sundari, C., Author and B. Prasad Babu and Digumarti Bhaskara Rao, Editors (2008). *Stress Among Pregnant Women*. New Delhi: Discovery Publishing House Pvt. Ltd. ISBN 978-81-8356-316-1.

Naga Kumari, U., Author and Digumarti Bhaskara Rao, Editor (2008). *Science Process Skills of School Students*. New Delhi: Discovery Publishing House Pvt. Ltd. ISBN 978 81 8356 263 8.

Nageswara Rao, S. and M. Srihari, Authors and Digumarti Bhaskara Rao, Editor (2004). *Guidance and Counselling*. New Delhi: Discovery Publishing House. ISBN 81-7141-840-6.

Nageswara Rao, S., Author and Digumarti Bhaskara Rao, Editor (2006). *Techniques of Teaching Psychology*. New Delhi: Discovery Publishing House. ISBN 81-8411-040-5.

Nageswara Rao, S. and P. Sridhar, Authors and Digumarti Bhaskara Rao, Editor (2004). *Methods and Techniques of Teaching*. New Delhi: Sonali Publications. ISBN 81-88836-33-8.

Nirmala Jyothi, M., Author and Digumarti Bhaskara Rao, Editor (2003). *Non-detention System in School Education*. New Delhi: Discovery Publishing House. ISBN 81-7141-654-3.

Padma Tulasi, G., Author and Digumarti Bhaskara Rao, Editor (2004). *Methods of Teaching Elementary Science*. New Delhi: Discovery Publishing House. ISBN 81-7141-871-6.

Pala Prasada Rao, V., Author and K. N. Rani and D. Bhaskara Rao, Editors (2004). *India Pakistan: Partition Perspectives in Indo English Novels*. New Delhi: Discovery Publishing House. ISBN 81-7141-871-6.

Pala Prasada Rao, V., Author and D. Bhaskara Rao, Editors (2008). *Functioning of Autonomous Colleges*. New Delhi: Discovery Publishing House Pvt. Ltd. ISBN 978-81-8356-258-4.

Pitchi Reddy, M., Author and Digumarti Bhaskara Rao, Editor (2007). *Techniques of Teaching Social Sciences*. New Delhi: Sonali Publications. ISBN 81-8411-066-X.

Prasad Babu, B., Author and P. Madhu and Digumarti Bhaskara Rao, Editors (2006). *Psychological Adjustment and Well-being*. New Delhi: Discovery Publishing House. ISBN 81-8356-204-3.

Prasad Babu, B., Author and M.V.R. Raju and Digumarti Bhaskara Rao, Editors (2006). *Behavioural Problems of School Children*. New Delhi: Discovery Publishing House. ISBN 81-8356-206-X.

Prabhakaram, K.S., Author and Digumarti Bhaskara Rao, Editors (1998). *Concept Attainment Model in Mathematics Teaching*. New Delhi: Discovery Publishing House. ISBN 81-7141-424-9.

Prasanth Kumar, J., Author and Digumarti Bhaskara Rao, Editor (1998). *Effectiveness of Distance Education System*. New Delhi: Discovery Publishing House. ISBN 81-7141-437-0.

Prasanth Kumar, J., Author and Digumarti Bhaskara Rao, Editor (2004). *Methods of Teaching Civics*. New Delhi: Discovery Publishing House. ISBN 81-7141-806-6.

Prasanth Kumar, J., Author and G. Sundara Rao and Digumarti Bhaskara Rao, Editors (2000). *Open University Student Support Services*. New Delhi: Discovery Publishing House. ISBN 81-7141-550-4.

Raja Kumari, M.A. and D.R.S. Sundari, Authors and Digumarti Bhaskara Rao, Editor (2004). *Special Education*. New Delhi: Discovery Publishing House. ISBN 81-7141-846-5.

Raja Kumari, M.A. and D.R.S. Sundari, Authors and Digumarti Bhaskara Rao, Editor (2004). *Methods of Teaching Educational Psychology*. New Delhi: Discovery Publishing House. ISBN 81-7141-820-1.

Rajeswari, S.M., Author and T. Santhanam, B. Prasad Babu and Digumarti Bhaskara Rao, Editors (2008). *Stress and Attitude of Women Teachers*. New Delhi: Discovery Publishing House Pvt. Ltd ISBN 978 81 8356 324 6.

Ramatulasamma, K., Author and Digumarti Bhaskara Rao, Editor (2002). *Job Satisfaction of Teacher Educators*. New Delhi: Discovery Publishing House. ISBN 81-7141-655-1.

Rama Krishnaiah, D., Author and Digumarti Bhaskara Rao, Editor (1998). *Job Satisfaction of College Teachers*. New Delhi: Discovery Publishing House. ISBN 81-7141-438-9.

Rama Kumar Ratnam, M.V., Author and Digumarti Bhaskara Rao, Editor (1998). *Dukkha: Suffering in Early Buddhism*. New Delhi: Discovery Publishing House. ISBN 81-7141-653-5.

Rama Krishna Prasad and P. Vide Sagar, Authors and Digumarti Bhaskara Rao, Editor (2004). *Methods of Teaching Physical Education*. New Delhi: Discovery Publishing House. ISBN 81-7141-868-6.

Rama Seshaiah, P. Author and Digumarti Bhaskara Rao, Editor (2004). *Methods of Teaching Home Science*. New Delhi: Discovery Publishing House. ISBN 81-7141-916-X.

Rama Swamy, K., Author and Digumarti Bhaskara Rao, Editor (2007). *Techniques of Teaching Environmental Science*. New Delhi: Sonali Publications. ISBN 81-8411-035-9.

Ramesh, A.R., Author and Digumarti Bhaskara Rao, Editor (2006). *Techniques of Teaching Commerce*. New Delhi: Sonali Publications. ISBN 81-8411-043-X.

Ramesh, Ghanta and Digumarti Bhaskara Rao, Editors (1998). *Environmental Education: Problems and Prospects*. New Delhi: Discovery Publishing House. ISBN 81-7141-423-0.

Ranga Rao, B., Author and Digumarti Bhaskara Rao, Editor (2007). *Techniques of Teaching Economics*. New Delhi: Sonali Publications. ISBN 81-8411-056-1.

Ranga Rao, R., Author and Digumarti Bhaskara Rao, Editor (2004). *Methods of Teacher Teaching*. New Delhi: Discovery Publishing House. ISBN 81-7141-812-0.

Rani, S.S., Author and Digumarti Bhaskara Rao, Editor (2006). *Techniques of Teaching Botany*. New Delhi: Sonali Publication: ISBN 81-8411-037-5.

Rathaiah, Lavu and Digumarti Bhaskara Rao, Editors (1996), *International Innovations in Education*. New Delhi: Discovery Publishing House. ISBN 81-7141-359-5.

Rathaiah, Lavu and Digumarti Bhaskara Rao (1997). *Achievement Correlates*. New Delhi: Discovery Publishing House. ISBN 81-7141- 385-4.

Ravi Krishna, M., Author and Digumarti Bhaskara Rao, Editor (2004). *Examination System*. New Delhi: Discovery Publishing House. ISBN 81-7141-824-4.

Ravi Kumar, M., Author and Digumarti Bhaskara Rao, Editor (2004). *Methods of Teaching Computer Science*. New Delhi: Discovery Publishing House. ISBN 81-7141-823-6.

Roja Ramani, V., Author and Digumarti Bhaskara Rao, Editor (2008). *Frustration of Prospective Teachers*. New Delhi: Discovery Publishing House Pvt. Ltd.

Rudramamba, B., Author and Digumarti Bhaskara Rao, Editor (2003). *Problems of Teaching*. New Delhi: APH Publishing Corporation. ISBN 81-7648-462-8.

Rudramamba, B. and V. Lakshmi Kumari, Authors and Digumarti Bhaskara Rao, Editor (2004). *Methods of Teaching Economics*. New Delhi: Discovery Publishing House. ISBN 81-7141-900-3.

Sambasiva Rao, P., Author and Digumarti Bhaskara Rao, Editor (2007). *Techniques of Teaching Psychology*. New Delhi: Sonali Publications. ISBN 81-8411-040-5.

Sanjeeva Rao, P.C., Author and Digumarti Bhaskara Rao, Editor (1996). *A Text Book of Geology*. New Delhi: Discovery Publishing House. ISBN 81-7141-313-7.

Santhanam, T., B. Prasad Babu and S. Sugandhi, Authors and Digumarti Bhaskara Rao, Editor (2007). *Children with Learning Disabilities*. New Delhi: Sonali Publications. ISBN 81-8411-077-4.

Santhanam, T., B. Prasad Babu and S. Sugandhi, Authors and Digumarti Bhaskara Rao, Editor (2008). *Learning Disabilities and Remedial Programmes*. New Delhi: Discovery Publishing House. ISBN 978-81-8356-257-7.

Sarala, M.M.O., Author and Digumarti Bhaskara Rao, Editor (2006). *Techniques of Teaching English*. New Delhi: Sonali Publications. ISBN 81-8411-047-2.

Satya Narayana, G., Author and Digumarti Bhaskara Rao, Editor (2008). *Attitude Towards Social Studies and Achievement in Social Studies*. New Delhi: Discovery Publishing House Pvt. Ltd. ISBN 978 81 8356 261 4.

Satya Narayana, V., Author and Digumarti Bhaskara Rao, Editor (2001). *Physical Education, Social Attitudes and Leadership Qualities*. New Delhi: Discovery Publishing House. ISBN 81-7141-593-8.

Satya Narayana, P.V.V. and G. Krishna, Authors and Digumarti Bhaskara Rao, Editor (2004). *Curriculum Development and Management*. New Delhi: Discovery Publishing House. ISBN 81-7141-813-9.

Shamsuddin, Sk. and V. Dayakara Reddy, Authors and Digumarti Bhaskara Rao, Editor (2007). *Academic Achievement and Values*. New Delhi: Discovery Publishing House.

Singh, Y.C., Author and Digumarti Bhaskara Rao, Editor (2006). *Techniques of Teaching Science*. New Delhi: Sonali Publications. ISBN 81-8411-041-3.

Sirisha Rani, S., Author and Digumarti Bhaskara Rao, Editor (2007). *Techniques of Teaching Botany*. New Delhi: Sonali Publications. ISBN 81-8411-037-5.

Sivaratnam Reddy, M., Author and Digumarti Bhaskara Rao, Editor (2004). *Creativity in College Students*. New Delhi: Discovery Publishing House. ISBN 81-7141-697-7.

Siva Lakshmi, G.V. and G.L. Subbaiah, Authors and Digumarti Bhaskara Rao, Editor (2004). *Methods of Teaching Environmental Science*. New Delhi: Discovery Publishing House. ISBN 81-7141-839-2.

Srinivas, G. and Digumarti Bhaskara Rao (2007). *Anxiety of Prospective Teachers*. New Delhi: Sonali Publications. ISBN 81-8411-084-7.

Srinivas, M. and I. Prasada Rao, Authors and Digumarti Bhaskara Rao, Editor (2004). *Methods of Teaching History*. New Delhi: Discovery Publishing House. ISBN 81-7141-803-1.

Srinivas Rao, P., Author and Digumarti Bhaskara Rao, Editor (2007). *Principles of Secondary School*. New Delhi: Sonali Publications. ISBN 81-8411-058-8.

Srinivasulu Reddy, M. and K.R.S. Sambasiva Rao, Authors and Digumarti Bhaskara Rao, Editor (1999). *A Text Book of Aquaculture*. New Delhi: Discovery Publishing House. ISBN 81-7141-482-6.

Srinivasa Rao, Mandalapu, Author and Digumarti Bhaskara Rao, Editor (2003). *Achievement Motivation and Achievement in Mathematics*. New Delhi: Discovery Publishing House. ISBN 81-7141-674-8.

Srihari, M., Author and Digumarti Bhaskara Rao, Editor (2003). *Values of Prospective Teachers*. New Delhi: Discovery Publishing House. ISBN 81-8356-328-7.

Subba Rao, K., Author and Digumarti Bhaskara Rao, Editor (2007). *School Education Policy*. New Delhi: Discovery Publishing House. ISBN 81-8356-285-X.

Subba Rao, K., Author and Digumarti Bhaskara Rao, Editor (2007). *Educational Planning*. New Delhi: Sonali Publications. ISBN 81-8411-053-7.

Sudhakar Reddy, Y., Author and Digumarti Bhaskara Rao, Editor (2003). *Creativity in Adolescents*. New Delhi: Discovery Publishing House. ISBN 81-7141-659-4.

Sunil Kumar, K. and K. Rama Krishana, Authors and Digumarti Bhaskara Rao, Editor (2004). *Methods of Teaching Chemistry*. New Delhi: Discovery Publishing House. ISBN 81-7141-913-5.

Suneetha, G., Author and Digumarti Bhaskara Rao, Editor (2004). *Environmental Awareness of School Students*. New Delhi: Sonali Publications. ISBN 81-8411-085-5.

Sunita, E. and R. Sambasiva Rao, Authors and Digumarti Bhaskara Rao, Editor (2004). *Methods of Teaching Mathematics*. New Delhi: Discovery Publishing House. ISBN 81-7141-915-1.

Suresh, K., Author and Digumarti Bhaskara Rao, Editor (2008). *Social Intelligence of Prospective Teachers*. New Delhi: Sonali Publications.

Surya Madhava, I., Author and Digumarti Bhaskara Rao, Editor (2006). *Techniques of Teaching Geography*. New Delhi: Sonali Publications. ISBN 81-8411-034-0.

Surya Madhava, I., Author and Digumarti Bhaskara Rao, Editor (2007). *Techniques of Teaching Political Science*. New Delhi: Sonali Publications. ISBN 81-8411-061-8.

Suvarna Raju, T.J.M., Author and M.V.R. Raju, B. Prasad Babu and Digumarti Bhaskara Rao, Editors (2008). *Personality and Adjustment of University Hostel Students*. New Delhi: Sonali Publications.

Swamy, K.R., Author and Digumarti Bhaskara Rao, Editor (2006). *Techniques of Teaching Environmental Science*. New Delhi: Sonali Publications. ISBN 81-8411-035-9.

Swarna Jyothi, K., Author and Digumarti Bhaskara Rao, Editor (2007). *Educational Research*. New Delhi: Sonali Publications. ISBN 81-8411-063-4.

Swarna Latha, C.D., and Digumarti Bhaskara Rao, Editors (2006). *Encyclopaedia of Biotechnology*, 5 Volumes. New Delhi: Discovery Publishing House. ISBN 81-8356-168-3.

Swarupa Rani, T. and J.R. Priyadarshini, Authors and Digumarti Bhaskara Rao, Editor (2004). *Educational Measurement and Evaluation*. New Delhi: Discovery Publishing House. ISBN 81-7141-859-7.

Vanaja, M., Author and Digumarti Bhaskara Rao, Editor (1999). *Inquiry Training Model*. New Delhi: Discovery Publishing House. ISBN 81-7141-515-6.

Vanaja, M., Author and Digumarti Bhaskara Rao, Editor (2004). *Methods of Teaching Physics*. New Delhi: Discovery Publishing House. ISBN 81-7141-867-8.

Valeri V. Koustiouk, Author and Digumarti Bhaskara Rao, Editor (2002). *A Text Book of Cryogenics*. New Delhi: Discovery Publishing House. ISBN 81-7141-642-X.

Vamsi Krishna, V., Author and Digumarti Bhaskara Rao, Editor (2004). *School Psychology*. New Delhi: Discovery Publishing House. ISBN 81-7141-880-5.

Veena Kumari, Balusu and Digumarti Bhaskara Rao (1996). *Operation Black Board*. New Delhi: APH Publishing Corporation. ISBN 81-7024-711-X.

Veena Kumari, Balusu, Author and Digumarti Bhaskara Rao, Editor (2004). *Methods of Teaching Social Studies*. New Delhi: Discovery Publishing House. ISBN 81-7141-899-6.

Veena Kumari, Balusu, Author and Digumarti Bhaskara Rao, Editor (2000). *Psycho-Social Correlates of Achievement*. New Delhi: Discovery Publishing House. ISBN 81-7141-547-4.

Venkata Rao, B., Author and Digumarti Bhaskara Rao, Editor (2007). *Techniques of Teaching Chemistry*. New Delhi: Sonali Publications. ISBN 81-8411-057-X.

Venkata Rao, P. and Digumarti Bhaskara Rao (1989). *A Text Book of Zoology*—Junior Intermediate. Guntur: Vignan Publishers.

Venkata Rao, P. and Digumarti Bhaskara Rao (1989). *A Text Book of Zoology*—Senior Intermediate. Guntur: Vignan Publishers.

Venkateswara Rao, V., Author and Digumarti Bhaskara Rao, Editor (2004). *Problems of Education*. New Delhi: Discovery Publishing House. ISBN 81-7141-841-4.

Venkateswara Rao, V., V.Vijaya Lakshmi and V. Vamsi Krishna, Authors and Digumarti Bhaskara Rao, Editor (2004). *Education For All*. New Delhi: Sonali Publications. ISBN 81-88836-30-3.

Venkateswara Rao, V., V. Vijaya Lakshmi and V. Vamsi Krishna, Authors and Digumarti Bhaskara Rao, Editor (2004). *Education in India*. New Delhi: Sonali Publications. ISBN 81-88836-858-9.

Venkateswara Reddy, L. and Narayana, M. L., Authors and Digumarti Bhaskara Rao, Editor (2004). *Education for Dalits*. New Delhi: Discovery Publishing House. ISBN 81-7141-872-4.

Venkateswara Reddy, L. and Narayana, M. L, Authors and Digumarti Bhaskara Rao, Editor (2004). *Methods of Teaching Rural Sociology*. New Delhi: Discovery Publishing House. ISBN 81-7141-811-2.

Venkateswarlu, K. and S.J. Basha, Authors and Digumarti Bhaskara Rao, Editor (2004). *Methods of Teaching Commerce*. New Delhi: Discovery Publishing House. ISBN 81-7141-808-2.

Venugopala Rao, K., Author and Digumarti Bhaskara Rao, Editor (2000). *Teacher Morale in Secondary Schools*. New Delhi: Discovery Publishing House. ISBN 81-7141-551-2.

Venugopala Rao, K., Author and Digumarti Bhaskara Rao, Editor (2007). *Techniques of Teaching History*. New Delhi: Sonali Publications. ISBN 81-8411-059-6.

Vidya, C., Author and Digumarti Bhaskara Rao, Editor (1996). *A Text Book of Nutrition*. New Delhi: Discovery Publishing House. ISBN 81-7141-309-9.

Vimala, T.D., B. Prasad Babu and Digumarti Bhaskara Rao, Editors (2007). *Stress, Coping and Management*. New Delhi: Sonali Publications. ISBN 81-8411-086-3.

Vijaya Bharathi, D., Author and Digumarti Bhaskara Rao, Editor (2000). *Educational Philosophies of Swami Vivekananda and John Dewey*. New Delhi: APH Publishing House. ISBN 81-7648-309-9.

Vijaya Bharathi, D., Author and Digumarti Bhaskara Rao, Editor (2005). *Educational Philosophy of John Dewey*. New Delhi: Discovery Publishing House. ISBN 81-8356-024-5.

Vijaya Bharathi, D., Author and Digumarti Bhaskara Rao, Editor (2005). *Educational Philosophy of Swami Vivekananda*. New Delhi: Discovery Publishing House. ISBN 81-8356-023-7.

Vijaya Lakshmi, D., Author and Digumarti Bhaskara Rao, Editor (2004) *Basic Education*. New Delhi: Discovery Publishing House. ISBN 81-7141-881-3.

Vijaya Lakshmi, V., Author and Digumarti Bhaskara Rao, Editor (2006). *Techniques of Teaching Music*. New Delhi: Sonali Publications. ISBN 81-8411-038-3.

Vijaya Kumar, S.J., Author and Digumarti Bhaskara Rao, Editor (2006). *Techniques of Teaching Mathematics*. New Delhi: Sonali Publications. ISBN 81-8411-039-1.

Visalakshi, V., Author and Digumarti Bhaskara Rao, Editor (2006). *Techniques of Teaching Biology*. New Delhi: Sonali Publications. ISBN 81-8411-045-6.

Visalakshi, V., Author and Digumarti Bhaskara Rao, Editor (2007). *Techniques of Teaching Zoology*. New Delhi: Sonali Publications. ISBN 81-8411-055-3.

Books in Telugu Language

Bhaskara Rao, Digumarti (1986). *Dhrushya Sravana Bodhanapakaranalu* (Audio Visual Teaching Aids). Guntur: Nagarjuna Publishers.

Bhaskara Rao, Digumarti (1993). *Jeevasashtra Bodhana* (Teaching of Biology). Guntur: Nagarjuna Publishers.

Bhaskara Rao, Digumarti (1995). *Vignanasasthra Bodhana* (Teaching of science) Guntur: Nagarjuna Publishers.

Bhaskara Rao, Digumarti (1997). *Vidya Manovignana Sastram* (Educational Psychology). Guntur: Creative Press.

Bhaskara Rao, Digumarti (1998). *DSC Study Material*. Guntur: Nagarjuna Publishers.

Bhaskara Rao, Digumarti (1998). *Upadhyayudu Vidya*. (Teacher and Education) Guntur: Nagarjuna Publishers.

Bhaskara Rao, Digumarti (1998). *Vidya Drukpadalu* (Perspectives of Education). Guntur: Nagarjuna Publishers.

Bhaskara Rao, Digumarti (1999). *EdCET Teaching Aptitude*. Guntur: Nagarjuna Publishers.

Bhaskara Rao, Digumarti (2001). *Bharata Samajamulo Upadyayudu Vidhya* (Teacher and Education in Emerging Indian Society). Guntur: Sri Nagarjuna Publishers.

Bhaskara Rao, Digumarti (2001). *Bhoutika Sastra Bodhana Padhatulu* (Methods of Teaching Physical Science). Guntur: Sri Nagarjuna Publishers.

Bhaskara Rao, Digumarti (2001). *Jeeva Sastra Bodhana Padhatulu* (Methods of Teaching Biology).Guntur: Sri Nagarjuna Publishers.

Bhaskara Rao, Digumarti (2001). *Vidya Manovignana Sastram* (Educational Psychology). Guntur: Sri Nagarjuna Publishers.

Bhaskara Rao, Digumarti (2003). *Patasala Yajamanyam/Paripalana* (School Management and Administration). Guntur: Sri Nagarjuna Publishers.

Gopala Krishna, G., A. Rama Krishna, K. Subba Rao and Bhaskara Rao, Digumarti (2004). *Jeevasashtra Bodhana Padhatulu* (Methods of Teaching of Biological science). Guntur: Sri Nagarjuna Publishers.

Krishna Murthy, V., K.S. Sudheer Reddy and Digumarti Bhaskara Rao (2004). *Vidya Manovignana Sastra Adharalu* (Foundations of Educational Psychology). Guntur: Sri Nagarjuna Publishers.

Lalini, V., V. Dayakara Reddy, M. Srihari and Digumarti Bhaskara Rao (2004). *Vidya Adharalu* (Foundations of Education). Guntur: Sri Nagarjuna Publishers.

Subba Rao, K.P., P. Ayodhya and Digumarti Bhaskara Rao (2004). *Patasala Yajamanyam - Vidhya Vyavasthalu* (School Management and Systems of Education). Guntur: Sri Nagarjuna Publishers.

Sudhakar, V., B. Ravindra Babu, D.S. Kumar and Digumarti Bhaskara Rao (2004). *Vidya Sanketika Sastram—Computer Vidhya* (Educational Technology and Computer Education). Guntur: Sri Nagarjuna Publishers.

Index

❑❑❑